LOOKING OUT FROM THE WINDOWS OF
My Soul

*Special Blessings
From
Maija The Poet*

By Maija The Poet

BG UNIVERSAL PRESS
Miami, Florida

....

REFERENCES & CREDITS

Copyright© 2023 by Mary Babun
All rights reserved.
ISBN-979-889074247-6

Unless otherwise indicated, Scripture quotations are taken from the Holy Bible,
New International Version®, NIV®. Copyright© 1973, 1978, 1984 by International Bible Society.
Used by permission of Zondervan. All rights reserved.

Many of the inspirations of the author comes from his devotional times while using My Utmost For His Highest,
The Golden Book of Oswald Chambers, Discovery House Publishers
Copyright© 1963. All rights reserved.

CONTENTS

I CALL HIM FATHER 1
MY EVERYTHING 3
YOU, THEY, SO, BUT 5
WALKING 9
LET ALL THAT IS IN ME PHRASE THE LORD 11
OUT OF EGYPT 13
BE OF GOOD COURAGE 15
REMEMBER ME 17
ON THE CROSS 19
HIDE IN YOUR CHAMBER 21
HAPPY TO BE ME 23
MY FATHER 25
THE GREATEST GIFT 27
LADY 29
MY LOVE 31
ONE BY ONE 33
REJOICE IN ME 35
THE EMERGING WOMAN 37
THANK YOU, THANK YOU, THANK YOU 39
WALKING IN GOD'S WISDOM 41
44 YEARS 43
THE PATH OF WISDOM 45
YOU HAVE SET ME IN A SAFE PLACE 47
FLY MY CHILD 49
EVEN ME 51
I HAVE FEET OF CLAY 53
IN PAIN 55
IT IS NOT ME BUT GOD 58
LISTEN TO YOUR TEARS 59
MOTHER 61
ON GOING PROBLEMS? 63
RUNNING AWAY 65
THANK GOD GLADY 67
THE MASTERS TOUCH 69
TODAY 71
WELCOME BACK 73
FEAR GOD 75
UNITED WE STAND 77
AFTER YOU HAVE SUFFERED 79
FEELINGS 81
BE CONTENT 83
EMBRACE FREEDOM 85
THE LORD IS MY HUSBAND 87
AS JESUS LOOKS DOWN 89

INTRODUCTION

Looking Out From the Windows of My Soul is a collection of very moving and inspirational personal moments of the author's life experiences as a Finnish American growing up in the 1960's in the "copper country" of Upper Michigan, to a life of a mature Christian mother and wife in the hustle & bustle of urban Miami, Florida.

Looking Out From the Windows of My Soul are quotable poems that readers will immediately identify with. They are daily life experiences that will encourage, uplift, and provide comfort to young girls, teenagers, young mothers, and grandmothers.

Looking Out From the Windows of My Soul will make you cry and laugh. But overall, this collection of comforting poems will help you become a better person and will bring you closer to God!

PREFACE

In this preface, I would like to share that for the past 26 years, I have dedicated myself to writing down my thoughts and ideas that arise during my moments of solitude with God and personal prayer. Over time, these thoughts evolved into poems that I felt compelled to share with my loved ones.

I Call Him Father

WHO IS IT WHO CREATED ME? IN MY MOTHERS WOMB? IT WAS HE, MY FATHER.
HE CREATED ME FOR HIS PURPOSES AND HIS PERFECT WILL.
TO LOVE HIM AND SERVE HIM AND BE HOLY SPIRIT FILLED,
TO SEEK HIS FACE, HIS VOICE, HIS HEART,
TO BE ONE IN HIM, AND NOT APART.

I CAN DO NOTHING APART FROM HIM,
MY LORD, MY SAVIOR, AND MY KING.
HE IS WITH ME ALWAYS, THIS, I AM SURE.
BECAUSE HE IN ME, IS MAKING ME PURE.
SO THAT I CAN ALWAYS GO THROUGH THIS LIFE AND ENDURE.
ALL THE HARDSHIPS AND INSULTS AND EVEN SLAMMED DOORS.

IT MAKES ME TO KNEEL DOWN AND BOW DOWN ON ALL FOURS.
TWO HANDS, TWO KNEES, FOR THE ONES THAT ARE LOST.
AS THEY DON'T REALIZE WHAT JESUS DID, AND AT WHAT COST.
HE DIED FOR ALL, FOR ALL OF OUR SINS,
IF ONLY WE TURN FROM OUR EVIL WAYS
AND REPENT AND LET HIM COME IN.

INTO OUR EMPTINESS, AND DECEPTIVE WAYS,
OPEN OUR EYES AND HEART LORD FOR THE REST OF OUR DAYS.
TO LIVE AT LAST, GET RID OF THE PAST.
TO BE FREE OF ALL SHACKLES, AND GUILT AND SHAME.
JUST SAY," FORGIVE ME LORD", MY FATHER, FOR THIS REASON YOU CAME.

TO LIVE ON EARTH AS A MAN, AND TO DIE AS MY SAVIOR, THAT WAS THE PLAN.
YOU DESTROYED DEATH, ONCE AND FOR ALL.
SO THAT WE WOULD BE READY, TO HEAR YOUR CALL.
"MY CHILD, I LOVE YOU, COME TO ME".
"I AM THE GREAT I AM"
YOUR FATHER…YOUR SET FREE!

IN JESUS NAME AND TO GOD BE THE GLORY!
Your daughter
Mary/Maija The Poet
Amen and amen.

My Everything

Are you looking for someone to be there for you all of the time?
When your low, when your happy, when your uncertain and don't know which way to go.

Someone who will love you through thick or thin, when your discouraged or wanting to give in.

When you feel your to do list is much to long, someone who could help you, who is also wise and strong.
Someone who isn't adding more, but comes along side, not with a chore, but with "Amor".

Amor is love and is uplifting. It makes you smile, it's a magnificent gift.
Well, let me introduce you to my everything.
He was born a man. He was despised, rejected, spit on and pierced on his side.
He was born to rescue us, is why he died.
He was our substitute for rebellion and sin, but we had no clue about sin, death, heaven or, hell. Until:

Until he opened our heart and our eyes to understand and be wise.
To ask him to forgive us of all our past, present, and future sin.
He is always waiting for us to call him.
To recognize him as our Savior, our Lord and our King.
His name is Jesus. My everything.
It is so easy to call upon his name. It was for this reason that Jesus came.
He was the substitute for us on that cross, he died for all mankinds sins,
For all nations and tongues.

He arose again, leaving us not alone, but with his Holy Spirit.
That's why there are so many songs to be sung.
Jesus loves me this I know, for the Bible tells me so.
Jesus is my Savior, my Lord and my King.
Now do you, see? "He is my everything"
I came by faith to God,
I repent of all my sins, past, present, and future.
I ask Jesus to accept me by faith.
To be my Savior, my Lord and my King.
"My Everything"

By: Maija The Poet

"You" "They" "So" "But"

YOU

YOU HELPED OUR ANCESTORS. YOU PLACED YOUR PEOPLE IN EVERY CORNER OF THE LAND.
YOU MADE THEIR DESCENDANTS AS NUMEROUS AS THE STARS IN THE SKY.
YOU BROUGHT THEM INTO THE LAND OF THEIR ANCESTORS.

THEY

THEY WERE DISOBEDIENT AND REBELLED AGAINST YOU.
THEY TURNED THEIR BACKS ON YOUR LAW.
THEY KILLED YOUR PROPHETS.
THEY COMMITTED TERRIBLE BLASPHEMIES.

SO

YOU HANDED THEM OVER TO THEIR ENEMIES.
THEY MADE THEM SUFFER.
BUT THEY CRIED TO YOU.
YOU HEARD THEM FROM HEAVEN.
YOUR GREAT MERCY.
YOU SENT THEM LIBERATORS WHO RESCUED THEM.

BUT

AS SOON AS THEY WERE AT PEACE,
THEY COMMITTED EVIL IN YOUR SIGHT.
YOU LET THEIR ENEMIES CONFUSE THEM.
THEY AGAIN CRIED TO YOU FOR HELP.
YOU LISTENED, IN YOUR MERCY,
YOU RESCUED THEM MANY TIMES.
YOU WARNED

THEY

BECAME PROUD AND OBSTINATE AND DISOBEYED YOUR COMMANDS.
THEY DID NOT FOLLOW YOUR REGULATIONS OR BRING LIFE IF THEY OBEY.
THEY STUBBORNLY TURNED THEIR BACKS ON YOU.
THEY REFUSED TO LISTEN.

YOU

YOU IN YOUR LOVE, WERE PATIENT WITH THEM.
YOU SENT YOUR SPIRIT, WHO WARNED THEM THROUGH THE PROPHETS.

BUT
THEY WOULD NOT LISTEN,

SO
ONCE AGAIN YOU ALLOWED THE PEOPLE OF THE LAND TO CONQUER THEM.

BUT
YOUR GREAT MERCY IN YOU DID NOT ALLOW THEM TO BE COMPLETELY DESTROYED,
OR ABANDON THEM FOREVER.

YOU
ARE A GREAT AND MERCIFUL AND GRACIOUS GOD.
YOU ARE MIGHTY AND AWESOME
YOU ARE UNFAILING IN YOUR LOVE.
YOU ARE JUST.

THEY
THEY THE LEADERS OF ALL DID NOT OBEY
OR LISTEN TO THE WARNINGS OR YOUR COMMANDS.
THEY DID NOT SERVE YOU, EVEN AS YOU I GAVE THEM KINGDOMS AND POWER,
THEY DID NOT SERVE YOU EVEN WHEN YOU SHOWERD THEM WITH GOODNESS UPON THEM,
YOU GAVE THEM ALL.
THEY REFUSED TO TURN FROM THEIR WICKEDNESS.

SO
NOW THEY ARE SLAVES. SLAVES TO THE KINGS,
LAND, LIVESTOCK. THEY SERVE THEM NOW AND THEY ARE IN GREAT MISERY.
"YOU" "THEY" "SO" "But"
GOD FORGIVE US ALL!!!!!!!!!!!!!!!!!!!!!!!
WHAT WRETCHED MEN, WOMEN AND CHILDREN ARE WE.
WHY DO WE ALWAYS HAVE TO BRAWL?
HELP US LORD TO FOLLOW YOUR CALL.
NOT FLEE?

BY: Maija The Poet

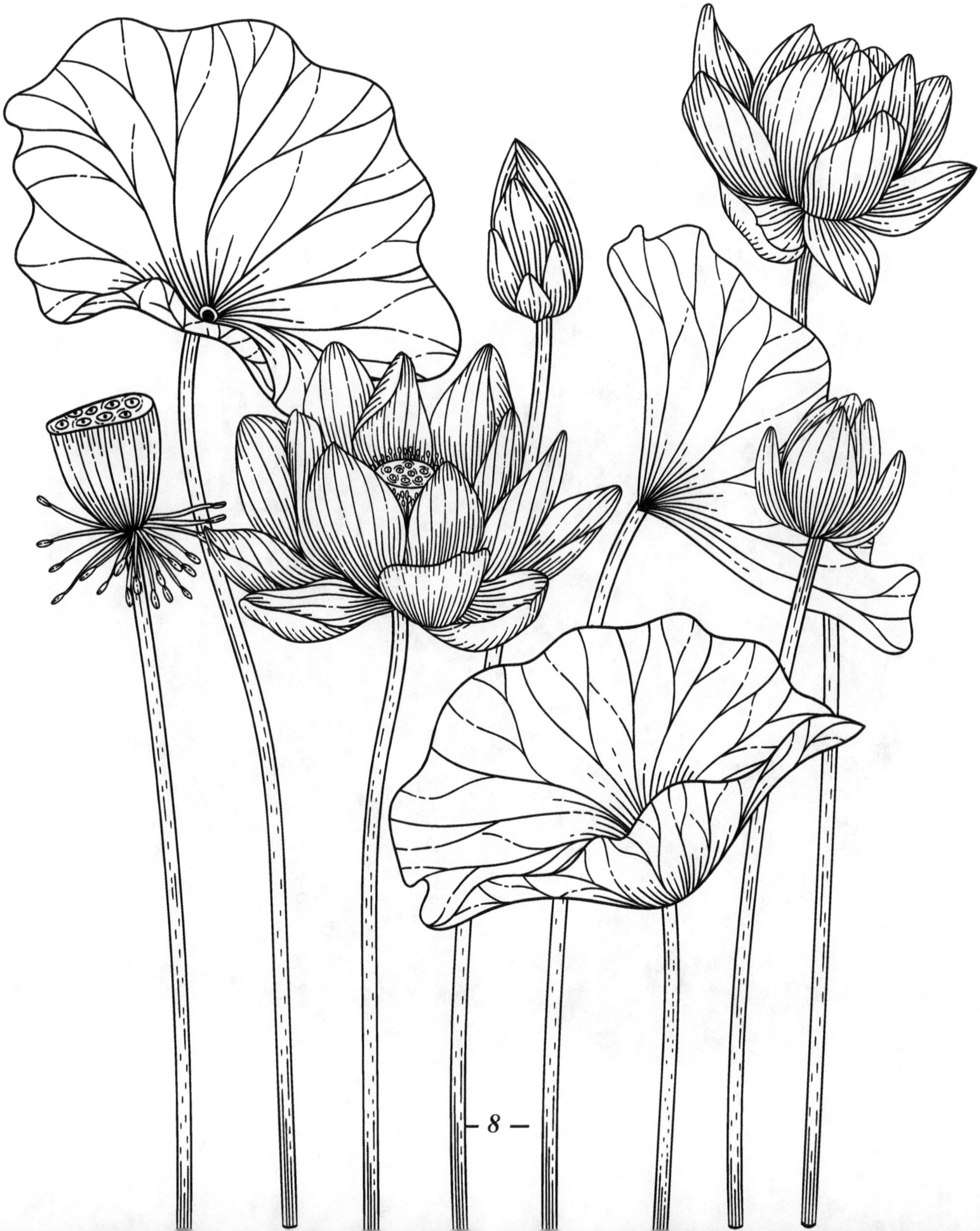

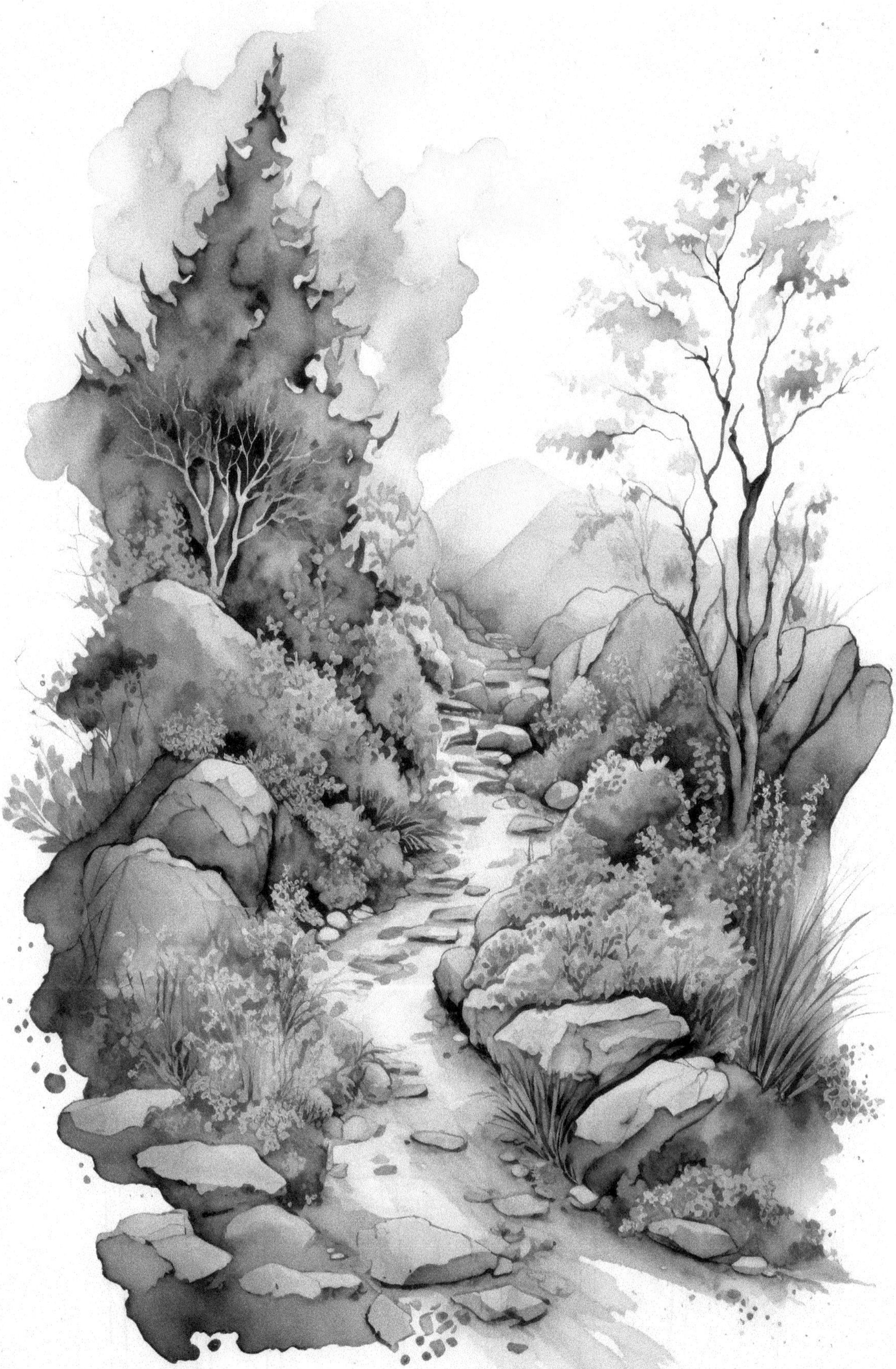

Walking

WALKING IN GOD'S WISDOM IS THE ONLY WAY TO LIVE
WE ARE SECURE AND HOPEFUL, IN OUR FUTURE, HE WILL GIVE.
IF WE DO NOT, WE WILL BE CUT SHORT OR STUNT OUR FUTURE,
THAT WOULD BE OUR LOT.

KEEP YOUR MIND ON THE RIGHT COURSE,
DRINKING AND OVEREATING MAKES ONE GROGGY AND FILLS YOU WITH REMORSE.
SELECT YOUR FRIENDS WISELY, AS THEY CAN LEAD YOU ASTRAY,
THEN YOU WON'T KNOW IF IT IS NIGHT OR DAY.

FATHER, I SUBMIT MYSELF TO YOU. PLEASE GRANT ME WISDOM,
SO THAT I WILL KNOW WHAT TO DO.
HELP ME TO BE UNDER YOUR CONTROL, SO THAT I CAN MEET EVERY GOAL.
EVERY GOAL YOU HAVE SET FOR ME, MAY IT COME TO PASS,
SO THAT I MAY BRING YOU GLORY AT LAST.

HELP ME TO THINK YOUR THOUGHTS. AND FOLLOW THEM THROUGH
SO THAT I SHALL LIVE AS I OUGHT AND GLORIFY YOU.
GRANT ME A SOUND MIND, IN ALL I THINK, SAY AND DO,
SO, I WILL MAKE THE RIGHT CHOICES AND AVOID WHAT IS UNTRUE.

MAY I BE FILLED WITH YOUR HOLY SPIRIT,
EVERY HOUR, EVERY MINUTE.
HELP ME TO LIVE A GODLY LIFESTYLE
ALL THE WAY TO THE LAST MILE.

TRULY, ETERNALLY YOURS FOREVER, TO GOD BE THE GLORY.

Maija The Poet

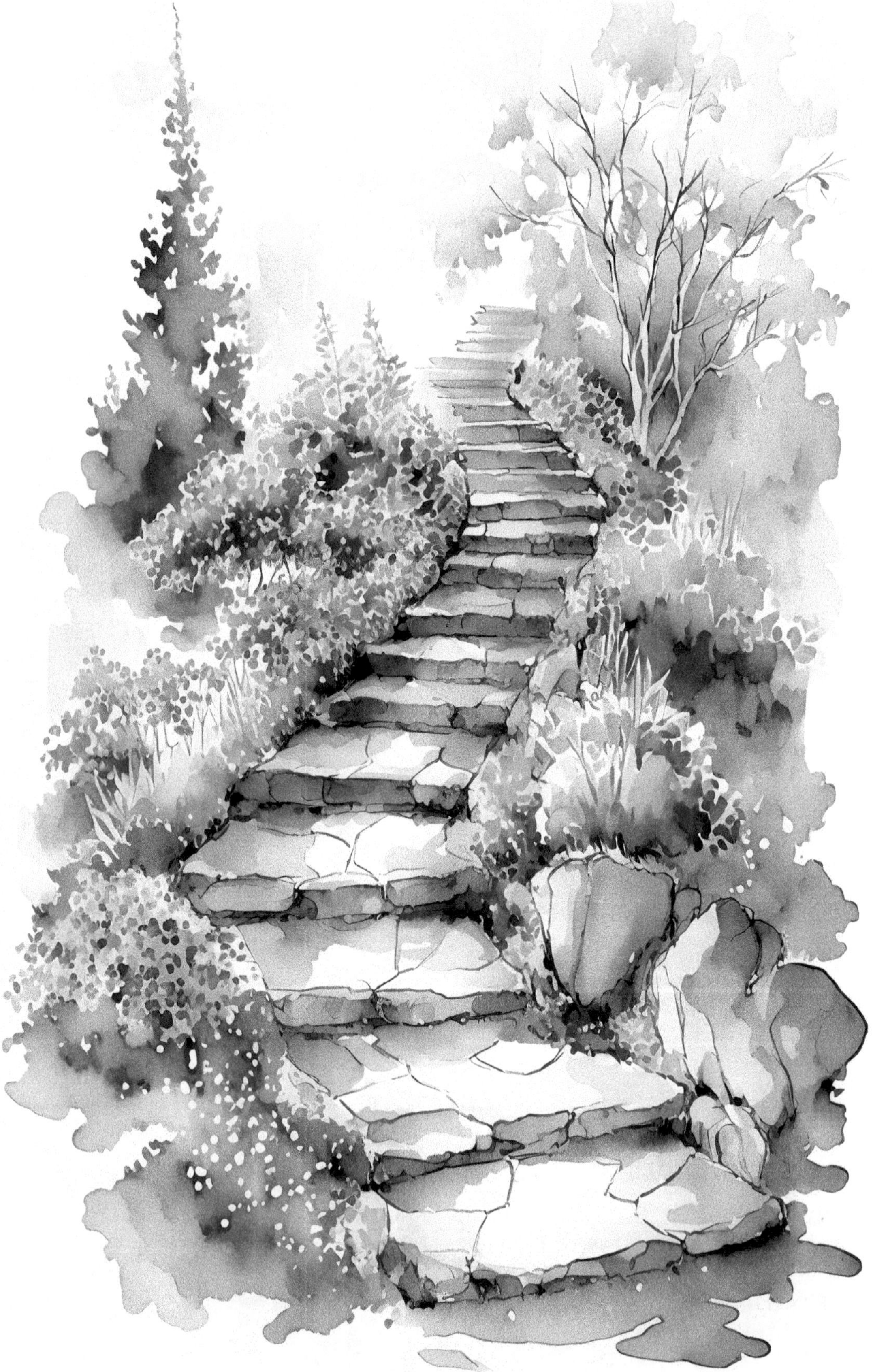

Let all that I am praise Him

When I wake up in the morning, I want to praise Him.
As I am walking through my day, I want to praise Him.
When I am driving in my car, and see the beauty of the sky, I want to praise Him.
When I see the beautiful deer and birds singing, I want to praise Him.

When I see the squirrels running up the trees, I want to praise Him.
When I see the numerous turkeys drinking from the waters, I want to praise Him.
When I see their chipmunks slurring across the road with nuts in their mouths, I want to praise Him.

Let all that is within me praise the Lord.

By: Maija The Poet

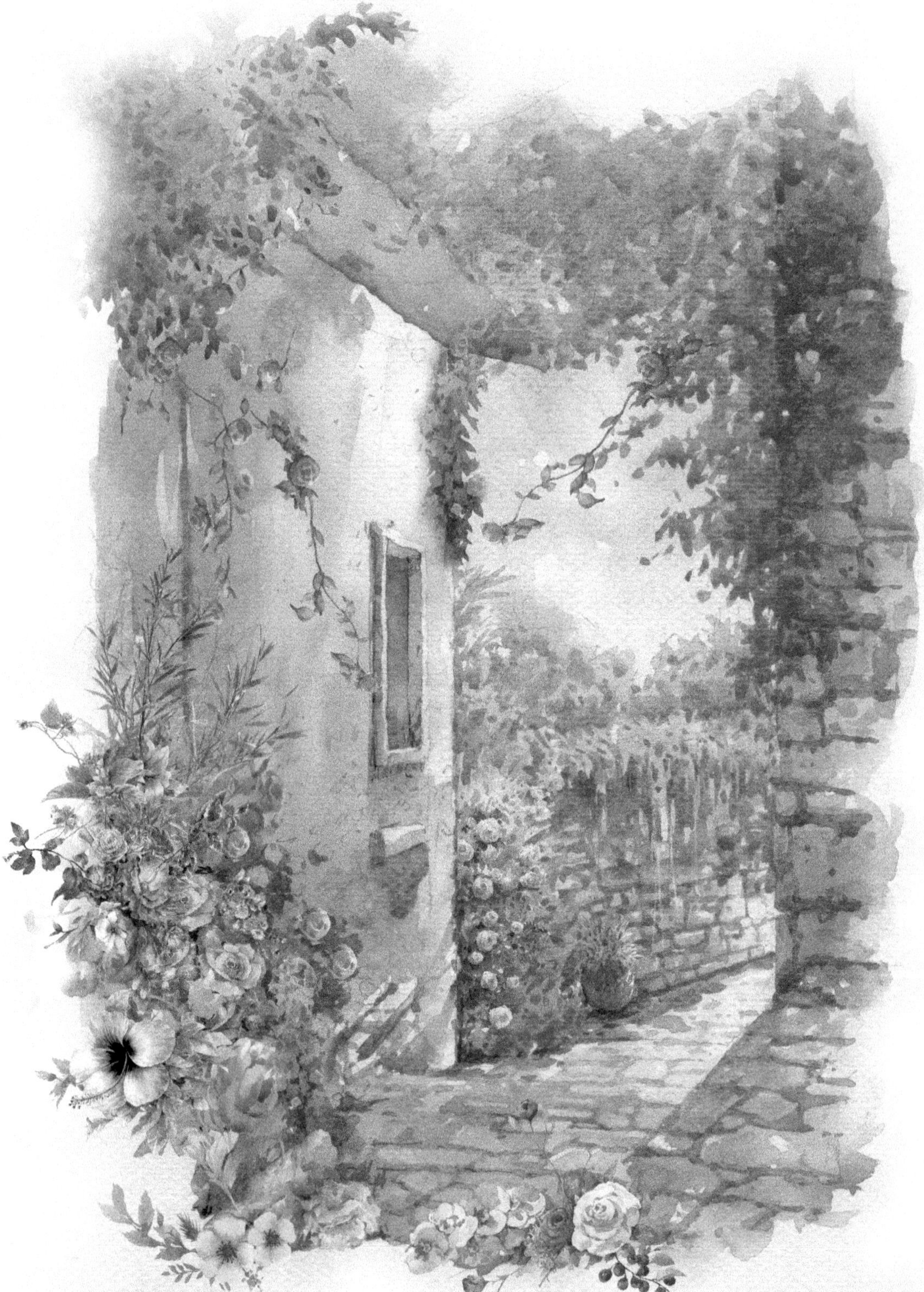

Out of Egypt

OUT OF EGYPT I DID COME. LED BY GOD TO BE RELEASED AS A SLAVE TO FREEDOM. LOST IN MY SIN, DID NOT KNOW IT WAS SIN, UNTIL GOD GAVE ME SALVATION, OPENED HIS DOOR AND LET ME IN.

SHOWED ME, I HAD IDOLS, RELIGION, NOT FREE
MANS WAYS, MANS THOUGHTS, TRADITIONS, AND RULES.
THERE WAS NO FREEDOM, JUST MANS WAYS AND CRUEL.
HE SHOWED ME HIS LOVE,
THAT CAME FROM ABOVE.
HIS SACRIFICE ON THE CROSS AS MY SIN AND ALL SIN TORTURED HIM, FOR HIS LOVE FOR ALL,
WAS NOT COUNTED AS LOSS.

HE WAS DEAD AND BURIED AS THE SCRIPTURES FORETOLD.
BUT THREE DAYS LATER, HE AROSE AGAIN, AS DEATH COULD NOT KEEP HIM.
MY SIN AND ALL SIN WAS NOW FORGIVEN.

HE IS ALIVE! MY SAVIOR MY KING, HE TOOK ME OUT OF EGYPT, AND NOW I CAN SING,
THANK YOU, LORD, FOR SAVING ME, FOR OPENING MY HEART, MY EYES TO SEE, THE TRUTH,
THE GOSPEL, THE ONE TRUE WAY.

IT IS FOR JESUS. I LIVE TODAY!
THANK YOU, LORD, FOR THEIR GIFT OF SALVATION.
IN JESUS NAME,
By: Maija The Poet

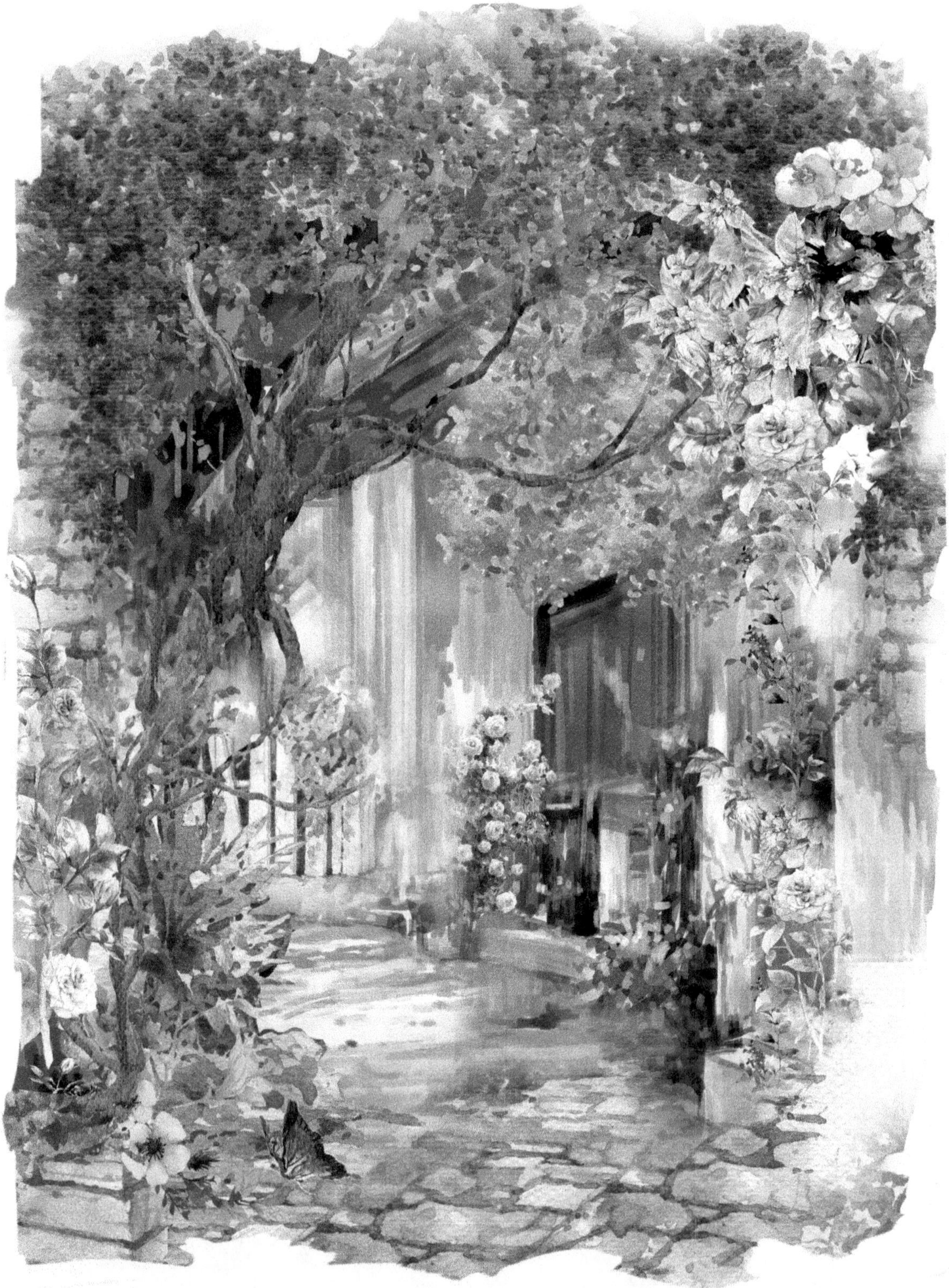

Be of Good Courage

Be OF GOOD COURAGE AND STAND STRONG WHEN....
THE BATTLE OF LIFE COMES YOUR WAY.

WHEN THE WORLDS WAYS TRY TO KEEP YOU AND TAKE YOU ASTRAY.
STAND STRONG AND BE OF GOOD COURAGE
FOR YOUR FATHER WILL HELP YOU ON YOUR WAY.

BE STRONG AND OF GOOD COURAGE WHEN YOUR FEELING LOW.
RAISE UP YOUR ARMS AND ASK GOD FOR HIS STRENGTH TO FLOW.
SAY NO TO THE NEGATIVES AND YES TO THE POSITIVES
FOR THE LORD OUR GOD SAYS, RISE UP, FOR I AM WITH YOU WHEREVER YOU GO.

THANK YOU, JESUS,
By: Maija The Poet

Remember Me

REMEMBER ME WHEN THINGS ARE GOOD
REMEMBER ME WHEN YOUR MISUNDERSTOOD
REMEMBER ME WHEN YOUR OUT AND ABOUT
THAT I AM ALWAYS WITH YOU, THERE IS NO DOUBT.

REMEMBER ME WHEN THE SKIES ARE GREY
REMEMBER ME WHEN YOU ARE ON YOUR WAY.
REMEMBER I AM WITH YOU ALWAYS EVERY DAY.
REMEMBER ME WHEN LOVED ONES PASS AWAY.
REMEMBER THEY ARE WITH ME, SLEEPING WHERE THEY LAY.

REMEMBER ME IN EVERY CIRCUMSTANCE OF LIFE
SIN HAS A WAY OF MAKING STRIFE
FEAR NOT, REPENT OF SIN. PRAY FOR ALL
BECAUSE SIN WAS THE REASON FOR THE FALL.

REMEMBER MY LOVE FOR YOU AND ALL, AS I WENT TO THE CROSS.
WILLINGLY I GAVE UP MY LIFE AND IT WAS NOT FOR LOSS.
REMEMBER ME, WHEN YOU SEE THE SON RISE.
AS I ALSO DID RISE, DON'T BELIEVE THE LIES.

I AM THE RESURRECTION AND THE LIFE.
WHOEVER BELIEVES IN ME WILL LIVE, EVEN THOUGH HE DIES,
AND EVERYONE WHO LIVES AND BELIEVES IN ME WILL NEVER DIE.
REMEMBER YOU WILL LIVE ETERNALLY IN HEAVEN WITH ME.
"REMEMBER ME"

IN JESUS LOVE AND NAME: Maija The Poet

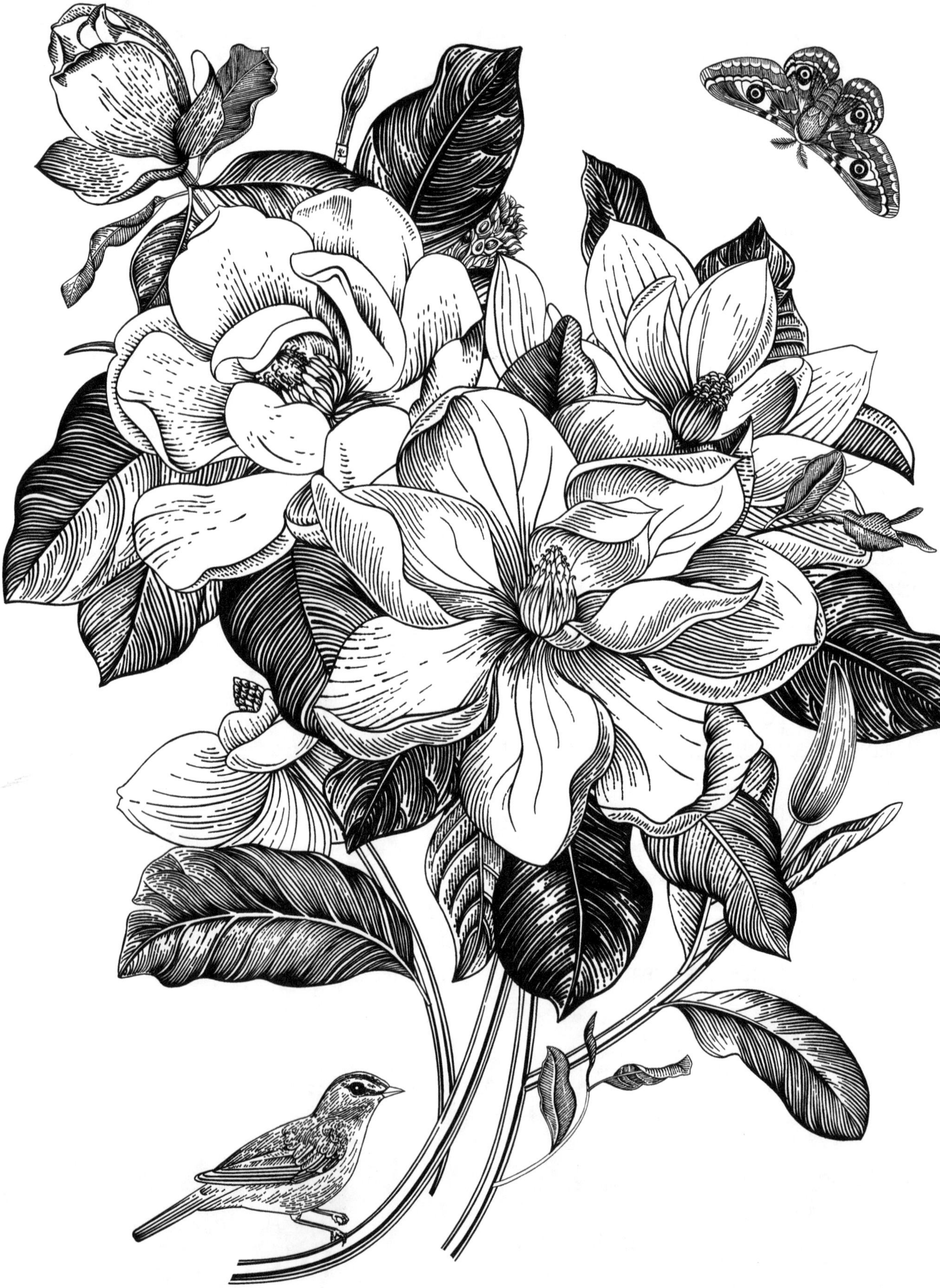

On The Cross

ON THE CROSS WITH JESUS,
I, A CRIMINAL DESERVING OF DEATH.
BUT NEXT TO ME HERE IS THIS MAN WHO HAS DONE NOTHING WRONG.
GIVING UP HIS LAST BREATH.

THE OTHER CRIMINAL SAID,
HE SAVED OTHERS, CAN'T HE SAVE HIMSELF?

THEN I SPOKE AND SAID,
DON'T YOU FEAR GOD EVEN WHEN YOU HAVE BEEN SENTENCED TO DIE?
WE DESERVE TO DIE FOR OUR CRIMES
NOT HIM, OH MY!

I THEN SAID, JESUS, REMEMBER ME WHEN YOU COME INTO YOUR KINGDOM.
THEN JESUS REPLIED,
TODAY, YOU WILL BE WITH ME IN PARADISE.
COME!
IN JESUS NAME AND LOVE.

Maija The Poet

Hide in your Chamber

I WILL WHISPER TO YOU THESE WORDS, GO NOW, HIDE IN YOUR CHAMBER
YOU SHALL BE SAFE THERE.

HARD TIMES ARE COMING AND DANGERS ARE AHEAD
BUT HIDDEN IN ME, YOU WILL REMAIN ALIVE AND NOT DEAD.

PRAY IN YOUR CHAMBER, THAT MANY WILL COME TO SALVATION.
BECAUSE SO MANY ARE LOST IN THIS NATION.

THEY CHOSE EARTHLY ITEMS, SEEKING ONLY MORE,
WHERE ETERNITY IS THE ANSWER
IT IS JESUS WHOM THEY NEED TO ADORE.

COME TO ME QUICKLY, TIME IS SO SHORT.
I LOVE YOU ALL SO DESPERATELY
OPEN YOUR EYES AND SHOW WITH A NOD.
REPENT OF YOUR SINS AND RETURN TO GOD.

I AM THE CREATOR OF YOU,
I MADE YOU; I LOVE YOU; I HAVE THINGS FOR YOU TO DO.
SO, COME TO THE SECRET CHAMBER
ALL BY YOURSELF.

JUST YOU AND ME,
TO TALK, TO LISTEN, TO PRAY, AND THEN OBEY.
HIDE IN YOUR CHAMBER, TIL I SAY TO COME OUT.
BECAUSE IN THE END, YOU WILL HAVE NO DOUBT.

THAT I AM THE TRUTH, THE LIGHT AND THE WAY.
TO GIVE YOU ETERNAL LIFE, FROM NOW ON AND EVERY DAY.

JUST LET GO, COME FOLLOW ME.
THEN YOU WILL SEE JESUS, AND BE FILLED WITH GLEE.

SAVED IN JESUS,
EMPOWERED BY THE HOLY SPIRIT
GIVING GLORY TO GOD THE FATHER
THE THREE IN ONE IS HE.

TO GOD BE THE GLORY

Maija The Poet

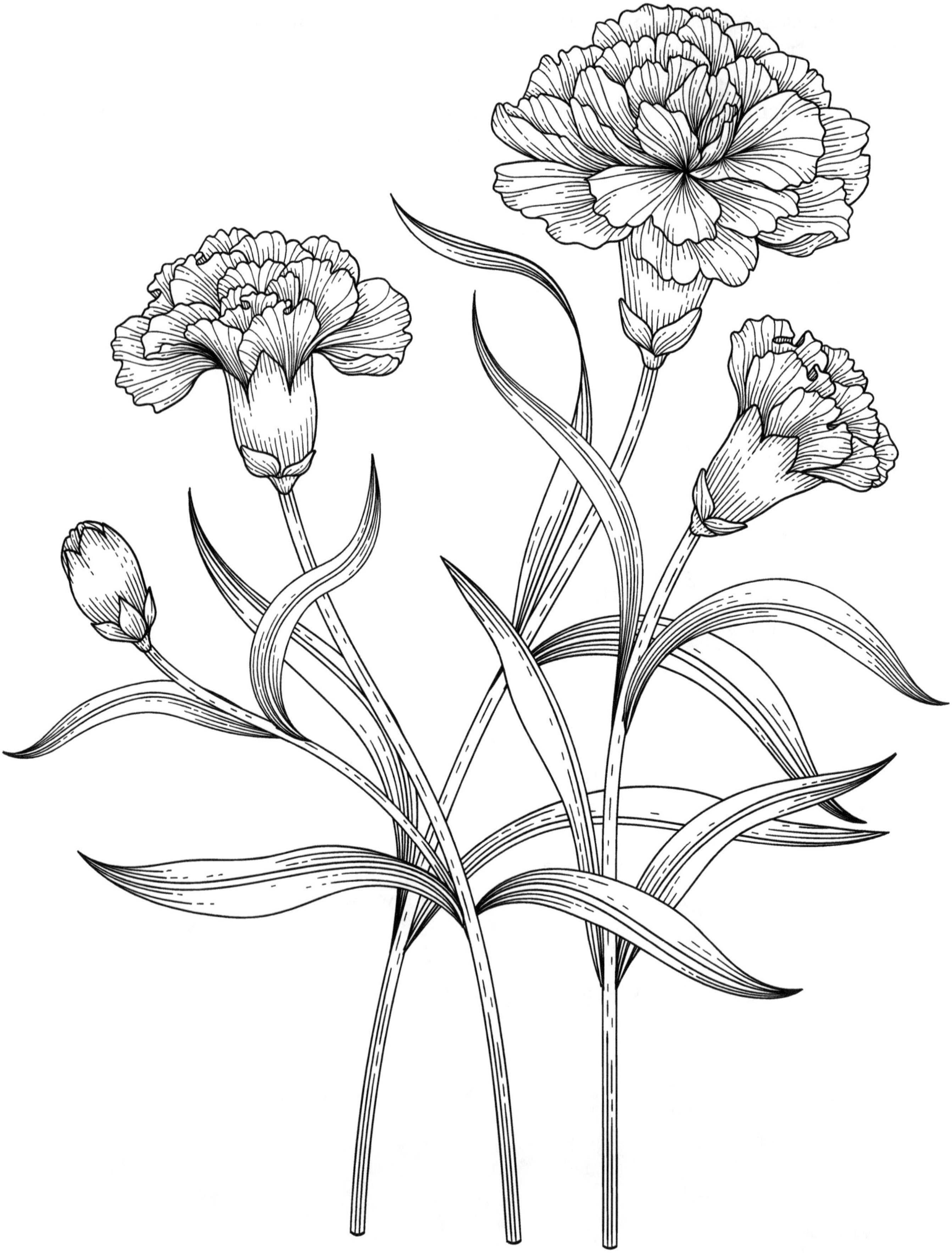

Happy to be Me

HELLO, HOW ARE YOU? I AM FINE, I HOPE YOU ARE TOO.
DID YOU WAKE UP THIS MORNING IN SPITE OF THE WORLDS NEWS.
WELL, JUST JUMP OUT OF BED AND COUNT YOUR BLESSINGS
MOVE OUT TODAY AND CONTINUE TO BELIEVE, THAT WE CAN HEAR, WALK, AND SEE.
SO TRULY BLESSED ARE WE.

I LIKE TO HUM AND SING OUT LOUD.
PRAISING GOD TO HIM, NOT THE CROWD.
MAY WE LEARN TO GIVE THE SACRIFICE OF THANKS.
NOT OUR TO DO LISTS OR BLOOD ANIMAL SACRIFICES.
ALL HE WISHES IS FOR US TO HAVE A HEART OF GRATITUDE.
NOT A "DO FOR ME SANTA CLAUS ATTITUDE."
HE DIED FOR YOU AND ME AND NOW WE ARE FREE.
FREE TO BE THANKFUL! THE CHAINS ARE GONE,
NO MORE STRIVING, GRACE FOR US ALL.
THANK YOU, FATHER, SON AND HOLY SPIRIT.

Maija The Poet

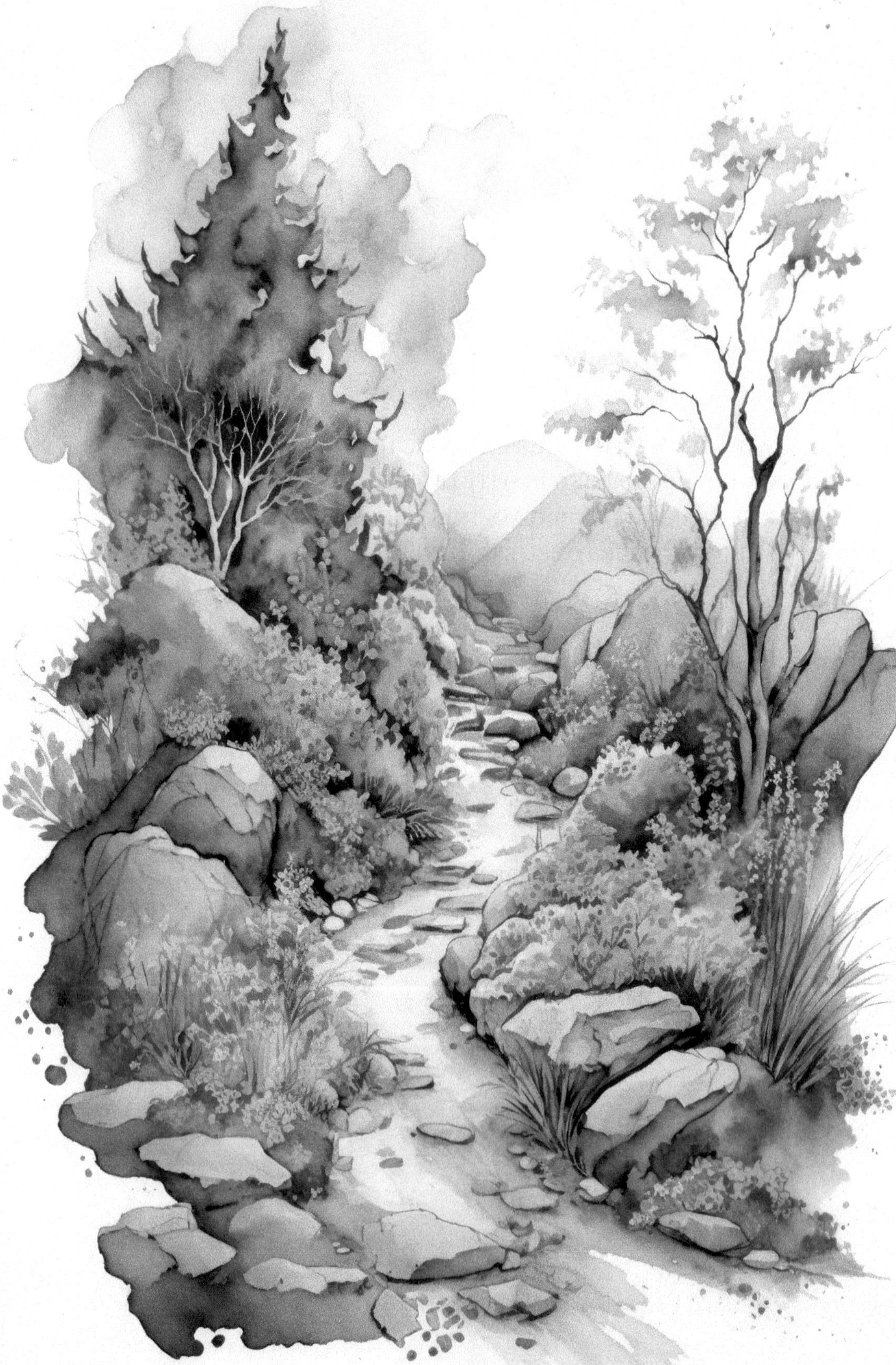

My Father

MY FATHER CREATED ME FOR HIS PURPOSE
WITH LOVING HANDS, AND NOT MUCH FUSS.
HE SPOKE THE WORD; HE BREATHED IN LIFE.

I WAS BORN FOR HIM, AS THE CORD WAS CUT WITH THE KNIFE.
FROM HEAVEN TO EARTH, I WAS SENT FROM HIM,
TO DO HIS WILL, HIS WAY, TO KEEP MY LIGHT BRIGHT, NOT DIM.
MY FATHER IS WITH ME WHEREVER I GO.
I FEEL HIS HAND ON MY SHOULDER, HIS LOVE I KNOW.
ALWAYS BESIDE ME, TO GUIDE ME EACH DAY.
TO STRENGTHEN ME, ENCOURAGE ME AND SHOW ME HIS WAY.
MY FATHER SENT JESUS TO ALL OF US ON EARTH.
TO LIVE FOREVER IN ETERNITY, NOW THERE IS REBIRTH.
FILL MY LIFE WITH YOUR WISDOM AND LOVE.

ONLY GODLY VIRTUES, THAT CAN ONLY COME FROM ABOVE.
EMPTY ME OF ALL FLESHLY WAYS.
FILL ME TO OVERFLOWING WITH YOUR SPIRIT, ALL OF MY DAYS.
FATHER, I LOVE YOU, THE THREE IN ONE.
THANK YOU FOR ALL THAT YOU HAVE DONE.
HELP ME TO SHOW OTHERS, HOW MUCH YOU CARE.
SO THAT WE CAN ALL MEET KING JESUS, IN THE AIR.

HAPPY FATHERS DAY

From Maija The Poet

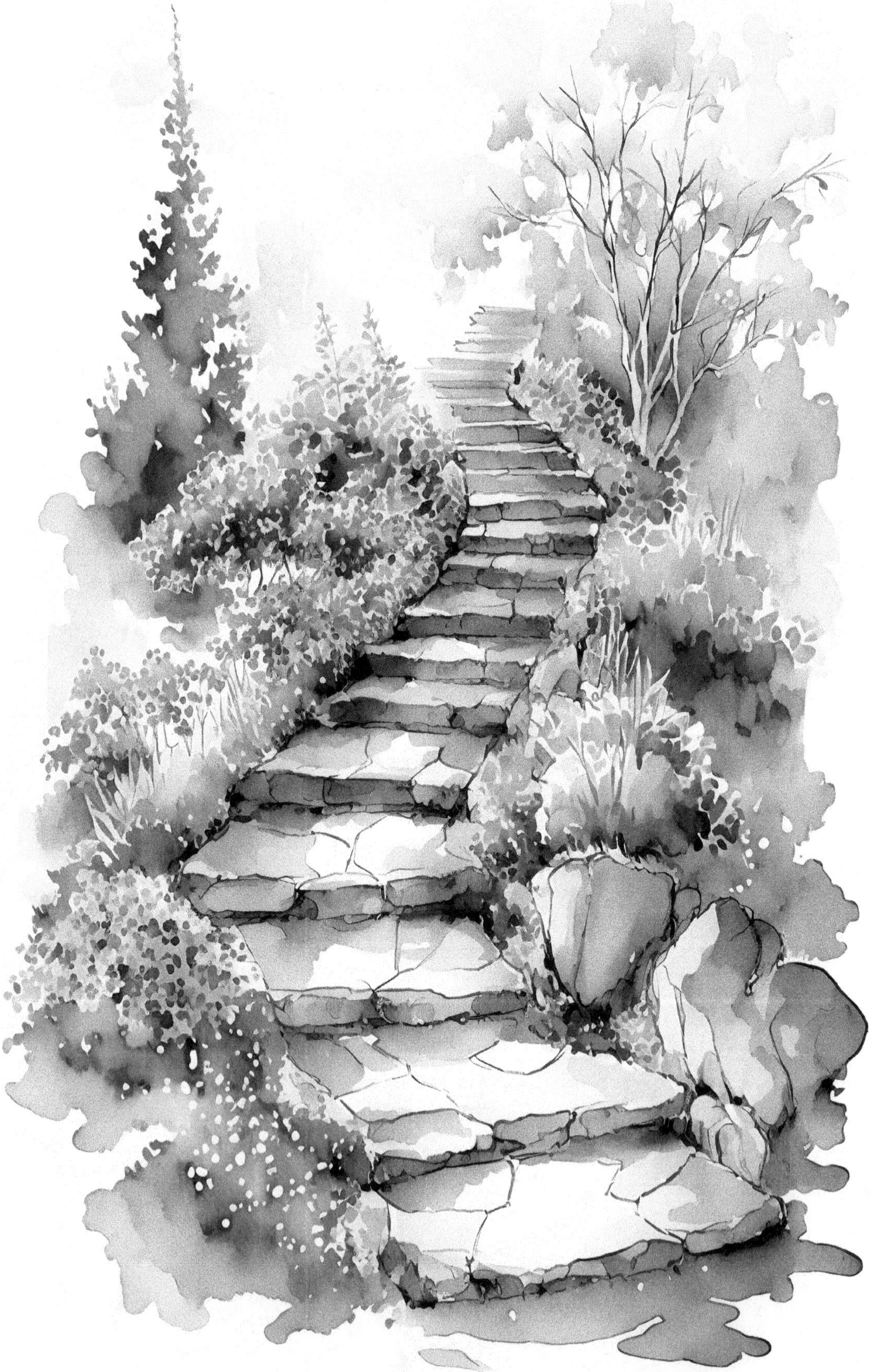

The Greatest Gift

THE GREATEST GIFT I HAVE EVER RECEIVED CAME FROM ABOVE.
WHEN I WAS A CHILD AND LEFT ON MY OWN,
IT WAS YOUR PRESENCE I FELT, YOUR EVERLASTING LOVE.
I NEVER FELT ALONE AS YOU WALKED ALONG WITH ME.
I TALKED, I SANG, I CRIED, I RAN TO YOU, THE GREAT "I AM" IS HE.
I SAW YOU IN THE HEAVENLY SKIES,
I SAW YOU IN THE SETTING OF THE SUN.
I SAW YOU IN EACH CHILD IN PLAY
I SAW YOU EACH AND EVERY DAY.

YOU WALKED WITH ME, YOU TALKED WITH ME.
YOU ALWAYS SHOWED YOUR WAYS FOR ME TO SEE.
YOUR WAYS ARE NOT MINE, OR OTHERS, THEY ARE THINE.
THE GREATEST GIFT TOO ME WAS TO BE INGRAFTED ON THE VINE.
THANK YOU, FATHER, THE GREATEST GIFT IS DIVINE.

"I AM THE VINE AND YOU ARE THE BRANCHES, APART FROM ME YOU CAN DO NOTHING".
JOHN 15:5

Maija The Poet/Mary Vincent Babun/MJB

Copyright Oct. 23, 2013

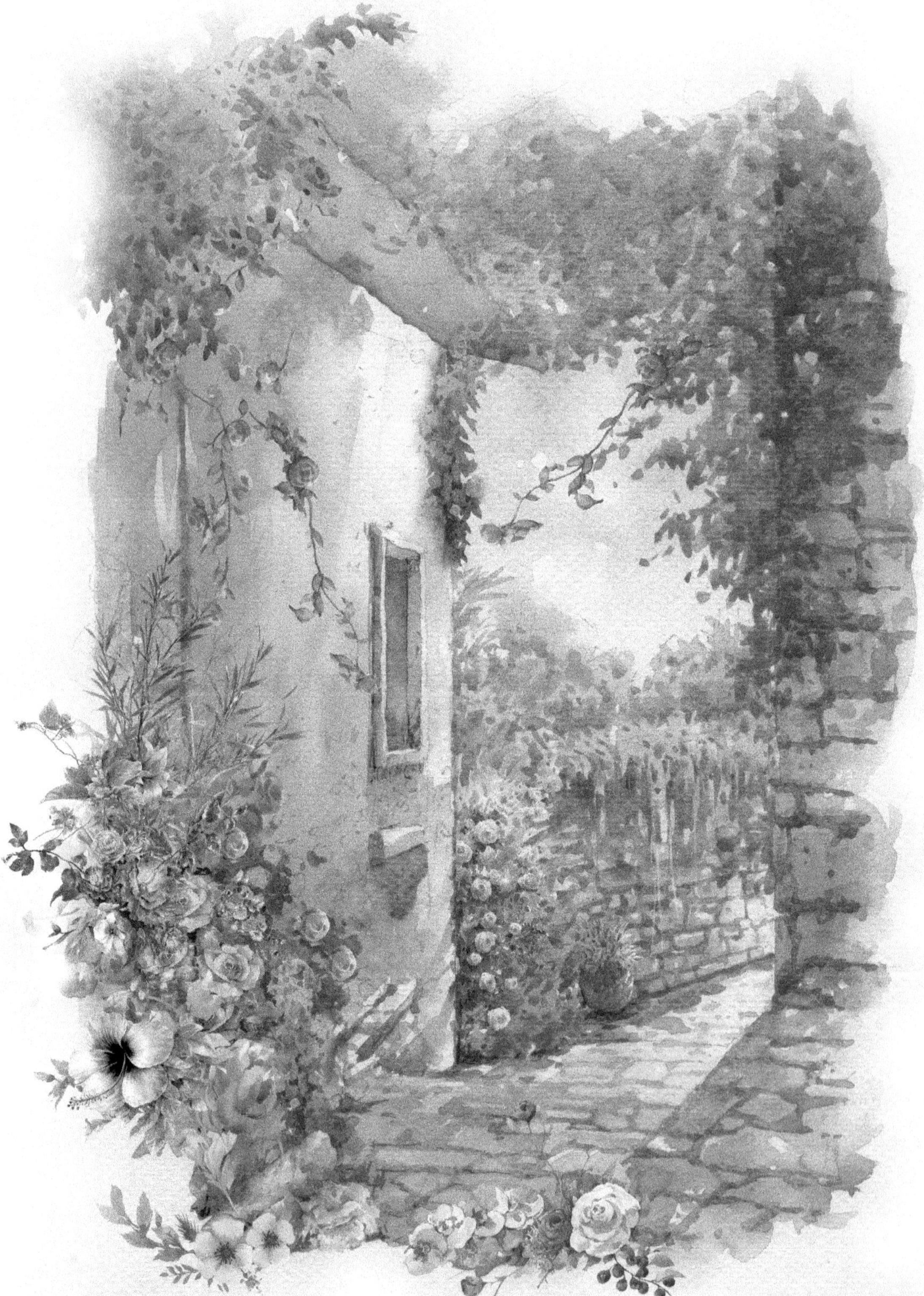

Lady

TREAT ME LIKE A LADY, EVERY TIME YOU ARE IN MY PRESENCE.
IT IS THE SOFTNESS, THE KINDNESS THAT COMPLIMENTS MY ESSENCE.
WHEN YOU ARE WITH ME, TREAT ME AS IF NO ONE ELSE IS THERE.
IT IS THROUGH YOUR LOVING ACTIONS, THAT SHOWS ME THAT YOU CARE.

DO YOUR EYES FOLLOW MY STEPS AS I SLOWLY SLIP AWAY,
OR DO YOUR EYES OFTEN GO ASTRAY?
WHEN YOU TREAT ME LIKE AN OLD DISH RAG,
TOSSING ME HERE AND THERE.

PUTTING YOUR NEEDS FIRST,
TELLS ME LOUDLY "YOU DON'T CARE".
HOW SOFTLY I FEEL, WHEN YOU TAKE THE TIME TO TOUCH.
MY BODY REACTS TO THE CHEMICAL REACTION,
IT DOESN'T REALLY TAKE MUCH.

IT DOESN'T TAKE MUCH TIME TO LET ME SEE,
THAT YOU REALLY ARE TAKING GOOD CARE OF ME.
A GENTLE MAN WITH A GENTLE WOMAN.
MAKE A LOVING PAIR.

HOW COULD THEY NOT LOVE EACH OTHER MORE
AS LOVE IS IN THE AIR.
TREAT HER LIKE A LADY, AND YOU WILL BE TRULY BLESSED.
IT ONLY TAKES KIND WORDS AND ACTIONS., AND YOU WILL BOTH DE STRESSED
ONE KIND WORD, ONE SWEET KISS, STARTS THE DAY OUT RIGHT, YOU WILL NEVER GO AMISS.

By: Maija The Poet. For Mothers Day. Mary J. Babun

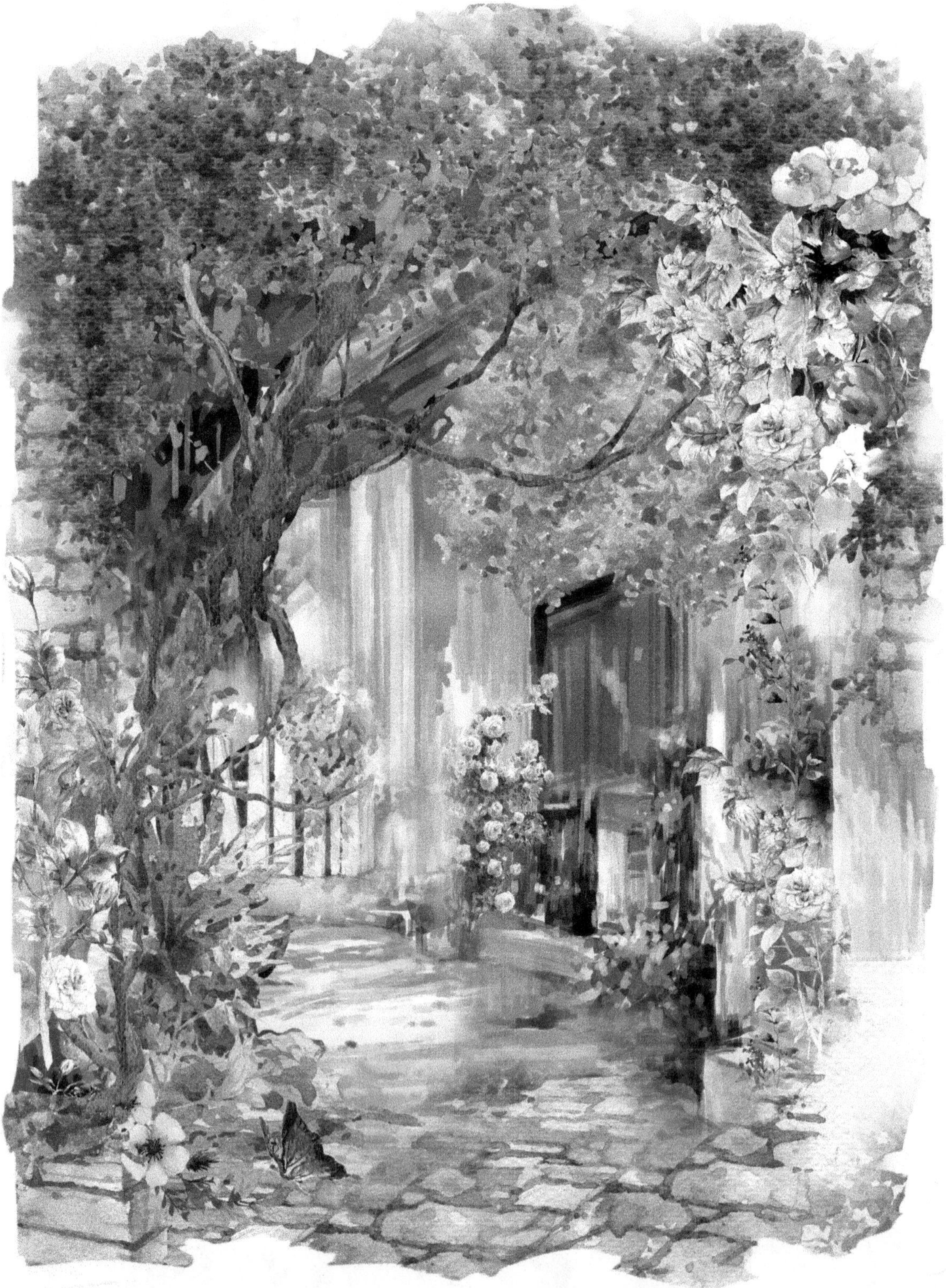

My Love

M IS FOR MYSTERY THAT IS WHAT YOU ARE TO ME,

Y IS FOR YEARNING THAT IS ME FOR YOU.

L IS FOR LOVING AS THAT IS HOW I WOULD LOVE US TO BE.

O IS FOR OUTINGS, EVERY FRIDAY NIGHT DATE, WE CAN DO.

V IS FOR VICTORIOUS, THIS RELATIONSHIP BETWEEN US TWO.

E IS FOR ETERNITY; I WANT TO SPEND THE REST OF MY LIFE WITH YOU.

By: Maija The Poet
Copyright

One By One

WE COME TO HIM ONE BY ONE, EACH ONE HEARS HIS VOICE AND THEN IT IS DONE.
TO BELIEVE OR NOT TO BELIEVE, IT IS UP TO EACH OF US TO RECEIVE.
THE WONDERFUL ETERNAL INVITATION GIVEN BY HIM TO THEE.
AS HE OFFERS THIS FREE GIFT OF ETERNAL LIFE, IT IS BY FAITH WE COME TO BE HIS WIFE.
AS HE IS THE GROOM AWAITING HIS BRIDE,
WILL MY FREE CHOICE MAKE ME FREE?
OR WILL IT BE PRIDE?
PRIDE TO THINK I CAN DO IT MY WAY, THROUGH MY WORKS, THROUGH SCIENCE,
RELIGION, THROUGH SACRIFICE AND GREAT PAY.

WHO REALLY KNOWS: HAVE THEY COME BACK TO TELL US; HE IS THE WAY?
OH YES, I RECALL LAZARUS AND THE RICH MAN, LAZARUS WENT TO HEAVEN,
THE OTHER WAS BANNED. SO NOW AS HE APPROACHES EACH ONE OF US,
ONE BY ONE, WHAT WILL YOUR DECISION BE?
WILL YOU ACCEPT GOD'S SON?

HE IS THE ONLY WAY, THE TRUTH AND THE LIGHT
I HOPE YOU SAY "YES". BEFORE THE END OF THE NIGHT."
NO, EQUALS DARKNESS FOREVER AND EVER.
YES, EQUALS LOVE, PEACE AND JOY AND ETERNAL LIFE AND THAT'S UNCONDITIONAL FOREVER.

THE FREE GIFT OF LIFE, HE OFFERS TO YOU.
THE GIFT OF FREE CHOICE, WHAT WILL YOU DO?
AS HE APPROACHES YOU IN HIS QUIET AND GENTLE WAY,
MAYBE YOU WILL ACCEPT HIM INTO YOUR HEART TODAY.
HE CALLED HIS DISCIPLES ONE BY ONE, AND IT IS THE SAME WAY TODAY.
"ONE BY ONE"

TO GOD BE THE GLORY WITH ALL THANKSGIVING
Copyright
By Maija The Poet/ MJB/Mary Vincent-Babun

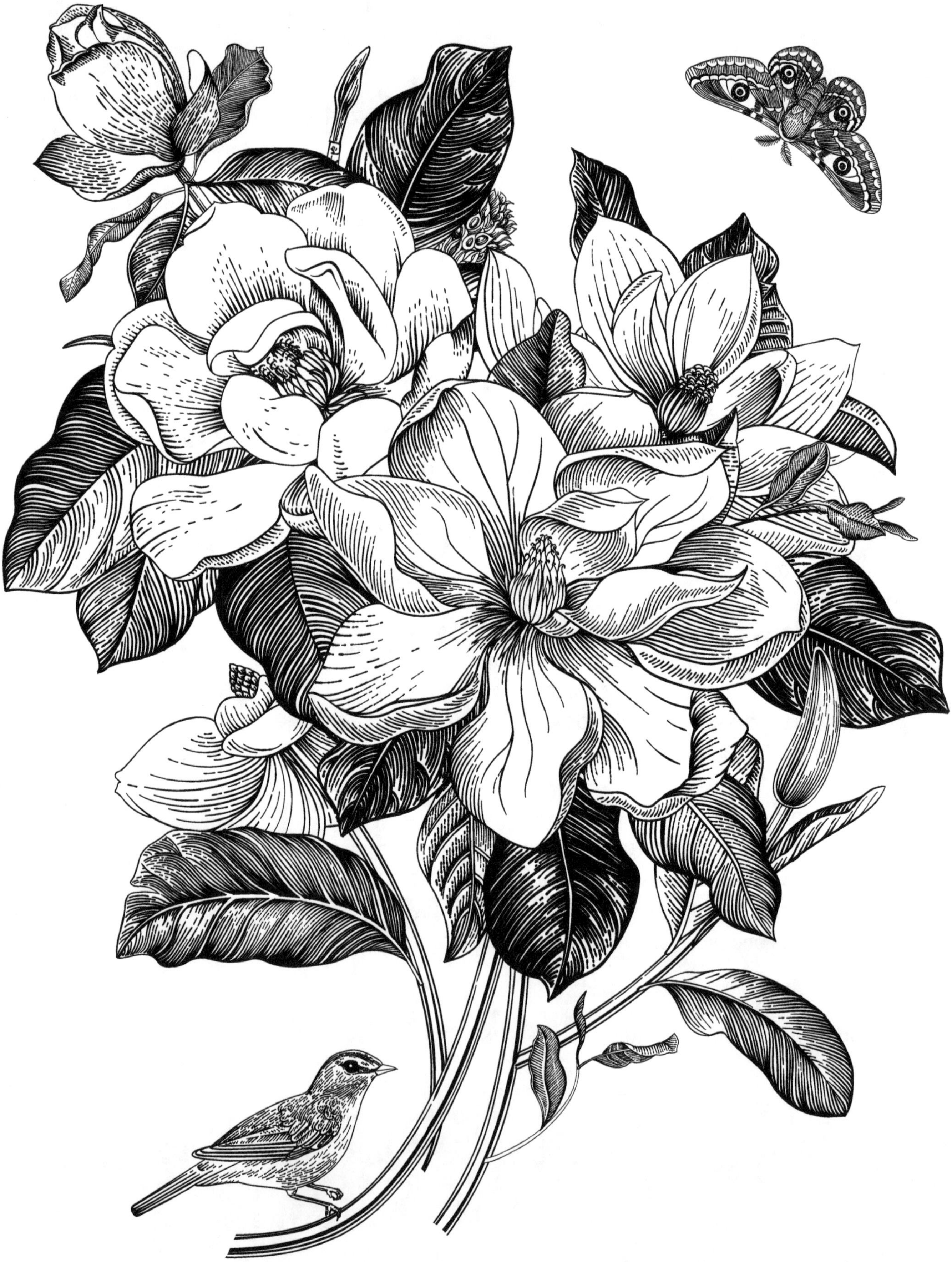

Rejoice in Me

REJOICE IN ME!!! YES LORD, I PRAISE YOU FOR YOU!
ALWAYS THERE. MY CONSTANT COMPANION AND FRIEND.
THERE IS NOTHING I CAN DO TO MAKE YOU FORGET ME OR UNLOVE ME,
EVEN UNTO THE END.

BEND ME, SHAPE ME, AND HELP ME TO FULFILL YOUR PURPOSE IN MY LIFE.
HELP ME TO OOZE OUT YOUR LIFE, YOUR LOVE IN ME TO OTHERS EVEN DURING DAYS OF STRIFE.
EVEN WHEN THOSE I LOVE SAY AND DO THINGS THAT CUT LIKE A KNIFE.
HELP ME TO PRAY FOR THOSE SO THEY TOO CAN RECEIVE ETERNAL LIFE.
AND WHEN THEY TURN THEIR LIVES TO YOU.
I WILL REJOICE WITH YOU BECAUSE IT IS TRUE
YOU ARE THE WAY, THE TRUTH AND THE LIFE. ALL WHO CAME TO YOU WILL SPEND ETERNITY
WITH YOU.

LET US REJOICE, LET US SING! FOR YOU MY LORD JESUS ARE EVERYTHING.

PS.92:2 "EVERY MORNING TELL HIM "THANK YOU FOR YOUR KINDNESS,"
AND EVERY EVENING" REJOICE IN ALL HIS FAITHFULNESS."

By Maija The Poet/ MJB/Mary Vincent-Babun

The Emerging Woman

I AM QUICKLY APPROACHING THE DATE, WHEN I WILL BE FIFTY-EIGHT.
I AM NOT AFRAID!!! I FEEL EXCITED!!! IT IS LIKE THE WOMAN INSIDE OF ME IS ABOUT TO EMERGE!!! POP OUT!!! EXPLODE WITH LIFE!!! SAY, "TA DA"!!!
WOMAN! I AM WOMAN!

WHAT'S NEXT? ENJOY THE MOMENT! AS I SIT ON MY BALCONY, I HEAR THE RUSTLE OF THE LEAVES AS THE PALM TREES SWAY TO AND FRO FROM THE STRENGTH OF THE WIND.

THE NOISE IS GETTING STRONGER AND LOUDER AS THE PITTER, PATTER OF RAIN NOW HAS TURNED INTO A TROPICAL STORM.

WHAT BEAUTIFUL SOUNDS! WHAT A BEAUTIFUL SIGHT!
A MOMENT TO SEE… TO FEEL… HEAR…AND ENJOY!
NATURE IN ITS FULL GLORY. GOD SPEAKING TO US.
REFRESHING THE EARTH. TURNING THE DRY SAND INTO SOILED SAND WITH A DEEPER COLOR.
BEING DRENCHED WITH RAIN, RIGHT BEFORE MY EYES.
THE PALM TREES CONTINUE TO SWAY AND SOAK UP THE RAIN AS IF TAKING A SHOWER.
THE PEALS OF THUNDER ENTER, HERE AND THERE.
THE COLOR OF THE OCEAN WENT FROM TEAL TO DARK GRAY TO DEEP BLACK.
THE BIRDS TAKE SHELTER AS THEY SEE THE APPROACHING STORM, THEIR WINGS FLAP HARDER AND FASTER TO GET AWAY AND SEEK REFUGE.
I TOO SHALL GO INSIDE NOW AS THE RAIN HAS REACHED MY DESTINATION MY OBSERVATORY.
MY CHAIR ON THE BALCONY.

THE RAIN IS LIKE MUSIC. IT MAKES ME FEEL CONTENT. LIKE I WANT TO CURL NAP WITH A BLANKET AND CONTINUE THIS MOST BLESSED MOMENT.
QUIET IS ALL AROUND ME, AS ALL ARE ASLEEP. ONLY THE MUSIC OF THE SOFT RAIN AS IT SLOWLY DRIFTS AWAY.

IT IS HARDER TO HEAR THE DROPS AND THE WIND, AS THE SUN IS BREAKING THROUGH.
THE EARTH. REFRESHED. CLEANSED FOR THE DAY…
MYSELF SO HAPPY THAT I WITNESSED A MIRACLE OF NATURE BEFORE ME.
TA DA!!! GOOD MORNING! ALL IS CALM.

By Maija The Poet/ MJB/Mary Vincent-Babun

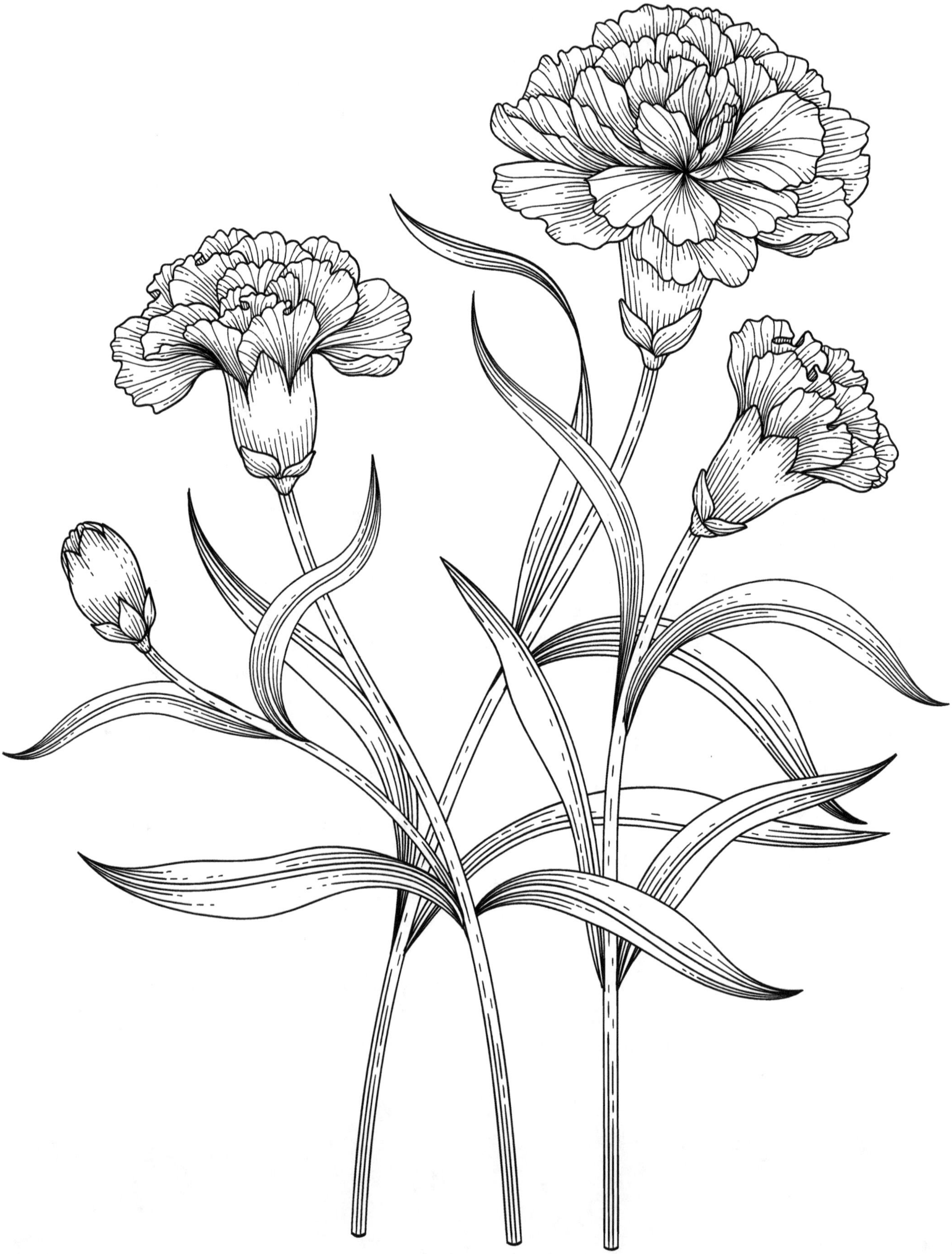

Thank you Thank you Thank you

THANK YOU, FATHER, FOR THE BEAUTIFUL TREES, THANK YOU FOR THE BEAUTIFUL LEAVES.
WATCHING THE LEAVES FALLING ONE BY ONE, UNTIL THE LAST ONE DROPS,
WE NOW KNOW THAT SUMMER IS ALMOST DONE.

THE COOL CRISP AIR, AS I TAKE IT ALL IN, SITTING IN MY CHAIR.
THE BIRDS ARE CHIRPING, THE HUMMINGBIRDS FLY BY,
TO SIP THEIR WATER, THEIR WINGS GO SO FAST, OH MY!
THE BUMBLE BEES AND WASPS STOP BY TOO.
LOOKING TO SEE HOW TO GET INTO THE BIRD FEEDER.
THEY CAN'T GET IN AND DON'T KNOW WHAT TO DO.

THE CLANG OF THE CHIMES IS MUSIC IN MY EARS.
AS THE WIND STIRS UP THE CHIMES FOR ALL TO HEAR.
THE RUSHING OF THE WATER AS IT GOES SWIFTLY BY THE CREEK.
I HOPE IT DOESN'T OVERFLOW AND START TO PEAK.

THE BIRDS ARE TWITTERING CALLING TO ONE ANOTHER,
AS I SIT ON MY CHAIR AT THE HOME OF MY SISTER AND BROTHER.
THANK YOU FOR THE WONDERFUL TIME,
TO BE ABLE TO SPEND WITH YOU, IT HAS TRULY BEEN SUBLIME.

THANK YOU FOR THE LAUGHTER AND STUDIES, BUT IT IS TIME TO GO.
YOUR FRIENDSHIP, YOUR LOVE, THE GOOD FOOD THAT WE ATE.
IS WHAT THE FATHER CALLS LOVE, NOW ISN'T THAT GREAT.
SO UNTIL WE SEE ONE ANOTHER AGAIN, STAY WELL, STAY CLOSE,
KEEP FOLLOWING HIM,
NEVER LET YOUR LIGHTS FLICKER NOR EVER GET DIM.
HE HAS A PURPOSE AND A PLAN FOR ALL OF YOUR LIVES.

IT IS HIS WORD, HIS WAY, HIS WILL THAT WE HAVE TO THRIVE.
I LOVE YOU WITH ALL OF MY HEART, BE BLESSED, PEACE TO YOU, NOW I MUST DEPART.
I LOVE YOU ALL, THANK YOU FOR YOUR LOVE AND CARE FROM THE BOTTOM OF MY HEART.

By Maija The Poet

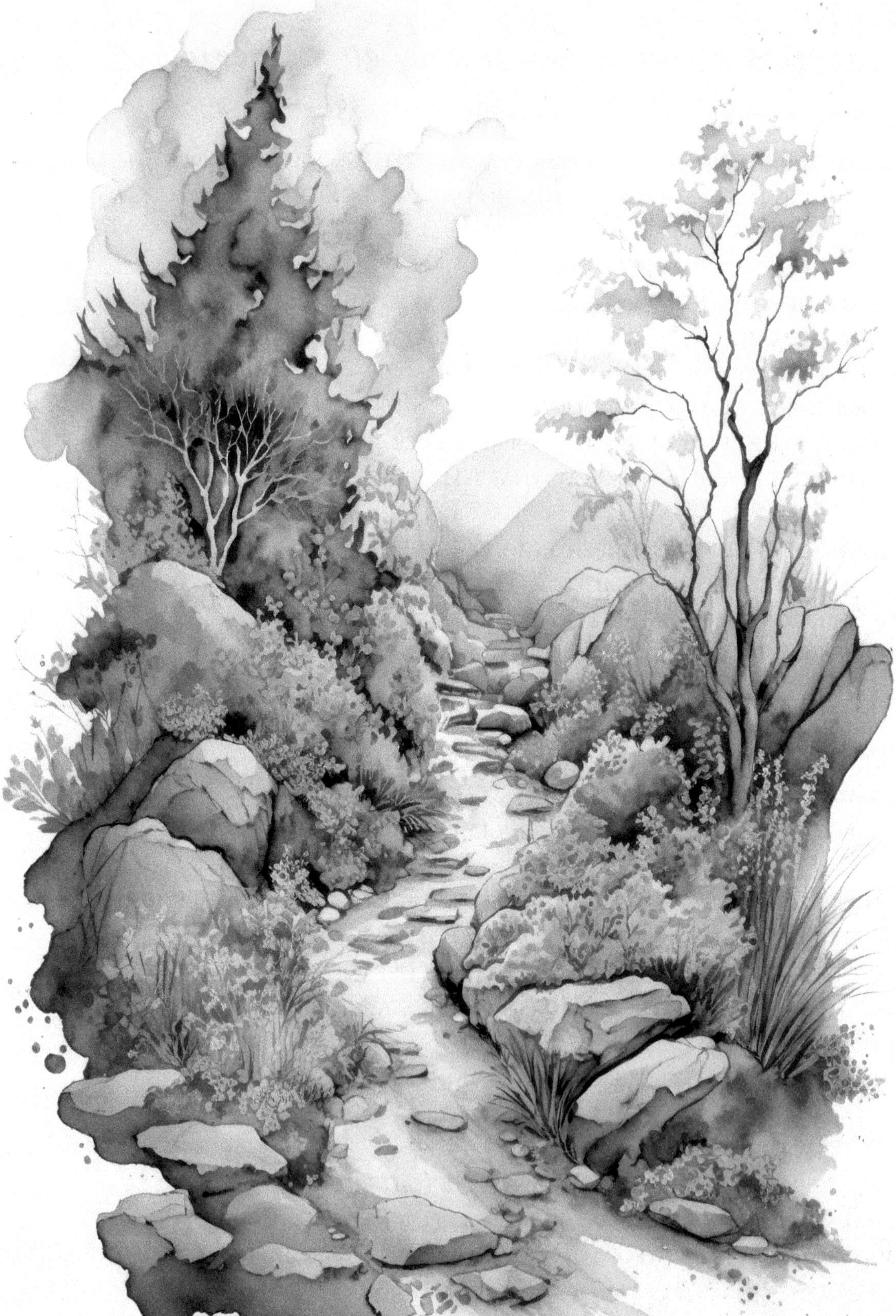

Walking in God's Wisdom

WISDOM IS THE ONLY WAY TO LIVE. WE ARE SECURE AND HOPEFUL,
IN OUR FUTURE, HE WILL GIVE.
IF WE DO NOT, WE WILL BE CUT SHORT OR STUNT OUR FUTURE THAT WOULD BE OUR LOT!

KEEP YOUR MIND ON THE RIGHT COURSE,
DRINKING AND OVEREATING MAKES ONE GROGGY AND FILLS YOU WITH REMORSE.

SELECT YOUR FRIENDS WISELY, AS THEY CAN LEAD YOU ASTRAY.
THEN YOU WON'T KNOW IF IT IS NIGHT OR DAY.

FATHER, I SUBMIT MYSELF TO YOU.
PLEASE GRANT ME WISDOM, SO THAT I WILL KNOW WHAT TO DO.

HELP ME TO THINK YOUR THOUGHTS AND FOLLOW THROUGH,
SO THAT I SHALL LIVE AS I OUGHT AND GLORIFY YOU.

GRANT ME A SOUND MIND, IN ALL I THINK, SAY AND DO.
SO, I WILL MAKE THE RIGHT CHOICES, AND AVOID WHAT IS UNTRUE.

MAY I BE FILLED WITH YOUR HOLY SPIRIT, EVERY HOUR, EVERY MINUTE.
HELP ME TO LIVE A GODLY LIFESTYLE.
ALL THE WAY TO THE LAST MILE..

TRULY, ETERNALLY YOUR FOREVER
YOUR DAUGHTER
From Maija The Poet

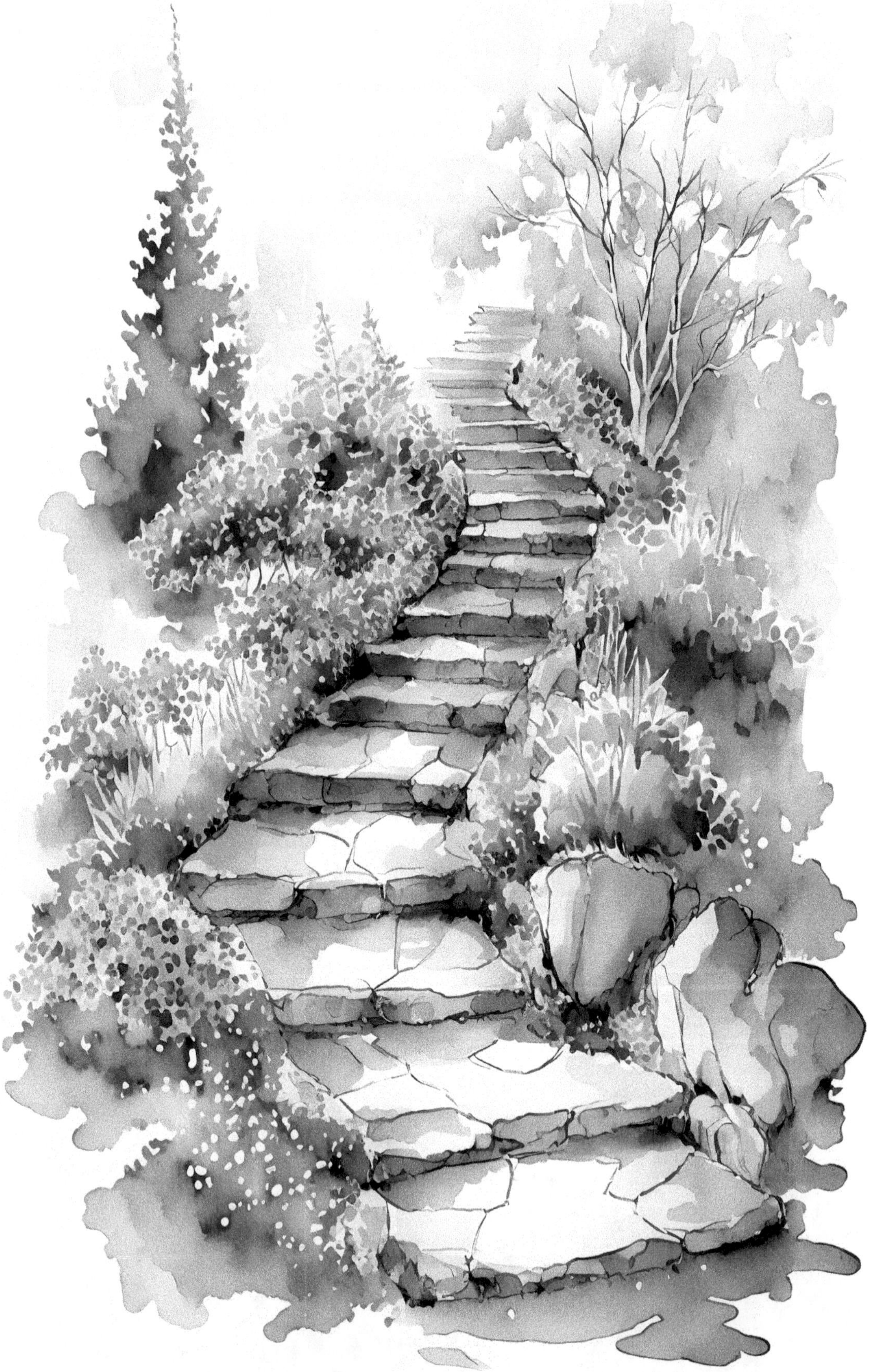

44 Years

44 YEARS AND HOPEFULLY MORE, I CANNOT BELIEVE WE ARE CELEBRATING 44.
WHERE DID THE YEARS GO, HOW DID THEY SLIP BY?
I WAS JUST A YOUNG THING, AND HE WAS THAT SPECIAL GUY.

TWO YOUNG PEOPLE FROM TWO DIFFERENT CULTURES.
TWO YOUNG PEOPLE, WOW! WHAT A MIXTURE.
ONE FRENCH, ENGLISH, ITALIAN, AND FINNISH, THE OTHER HISPANIC.
I THINK OUR PARENTS ACTUALLY DID PANIC.

BUT NOW WERE CELEBRATING OUR 55TH.
THE LORD HAS BEEN SO GOOD TO US
AND AS I WILL ALWAYS SAY, "GOD IS THE GLUE".
NOW HOW ABOUT YOU?

From Maija The Poet

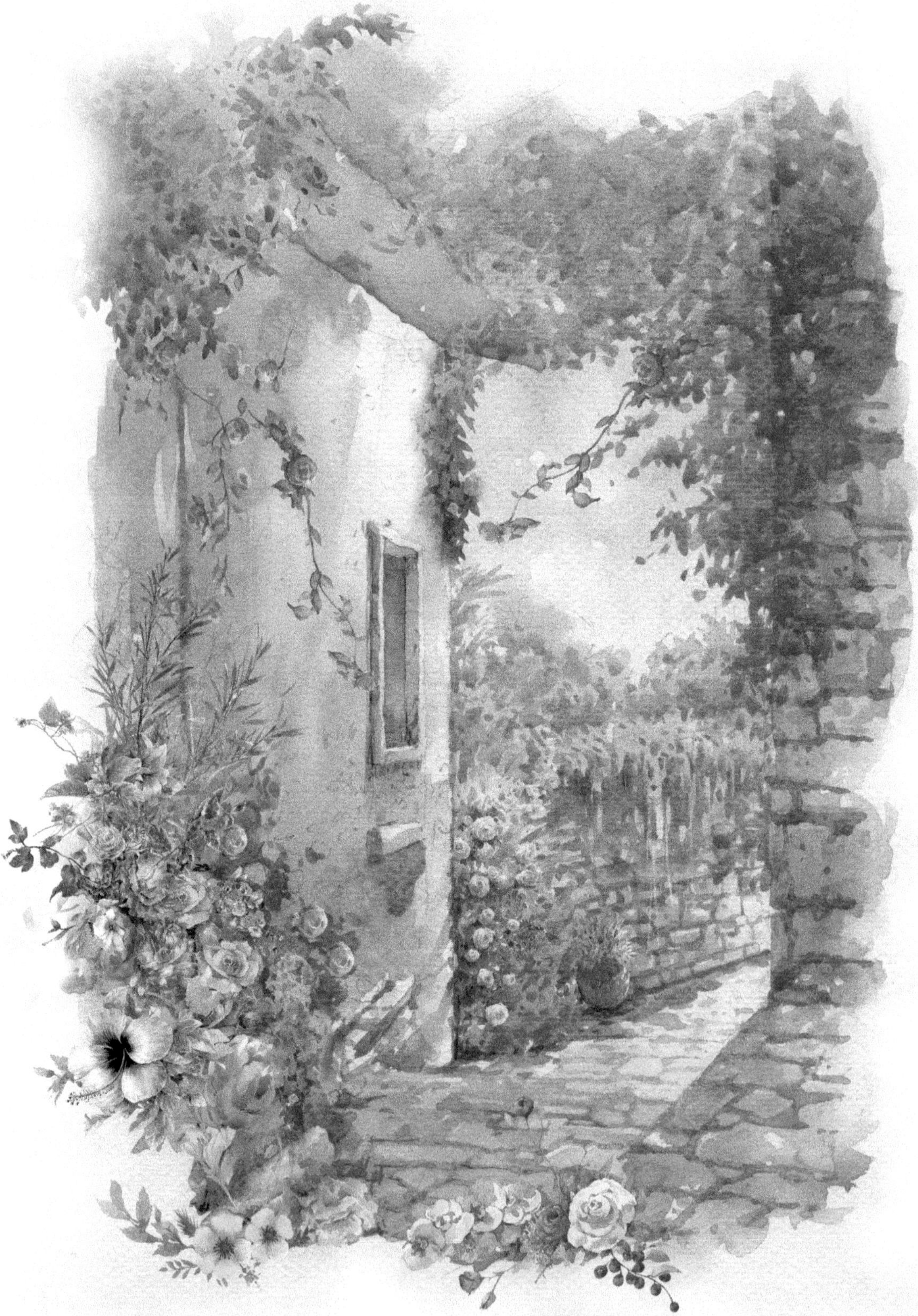

The Path of Wisdom

STEP ON THE PATH OF WISDOM, AND NEVER TURN BACK.
TAKE ONE STEP AT A TIME, THERE WILL BE JOY, NO LACK.

IT IS GOD'S WISDOM, GUIDED BY HIS HAND,
THAT WILL BLESS YOU WHEREVER YOU LAND.

PURSUING GOD'S WISDOM IS THE ONLY WAY TO GO.
TO KEEP YOU FROM BAD DECISIONS AND TOSSED TO AND FRO.

PURSUING GODLY WISDOM, RESULTS IN JOY.
EVEN WHEN HEARTACHE COMES, THE JOY COMES OUT.
AND WE KNOW WHERE IT COMES FROM.

HAPPINESS AND JOY ARE TWO DIFFERENT THINGS.
EVEN WHEN ONE PASSES THROUGH THE SHADOW OF DEATH AND OTHER OF LIFE'S STINGS.

GODLY WISDOM AND GODLY JOY.
DO NOT ALWAYS LINE UP WITH WHAT THE WORLD THINK IS WISE.

BUT KNOWING AND DONG WHAT IS RIGHT ACCORDING TO HIS WORD.
LEADS TO CONTENTMENT AND JOY AND NEVER DIES.

STAY ON THE PATH OF WISDOM, THE BEST IS YET TO COME.

IN JESUS NAME AND TO GOD BE THE GLORY

By: Maija The Poet

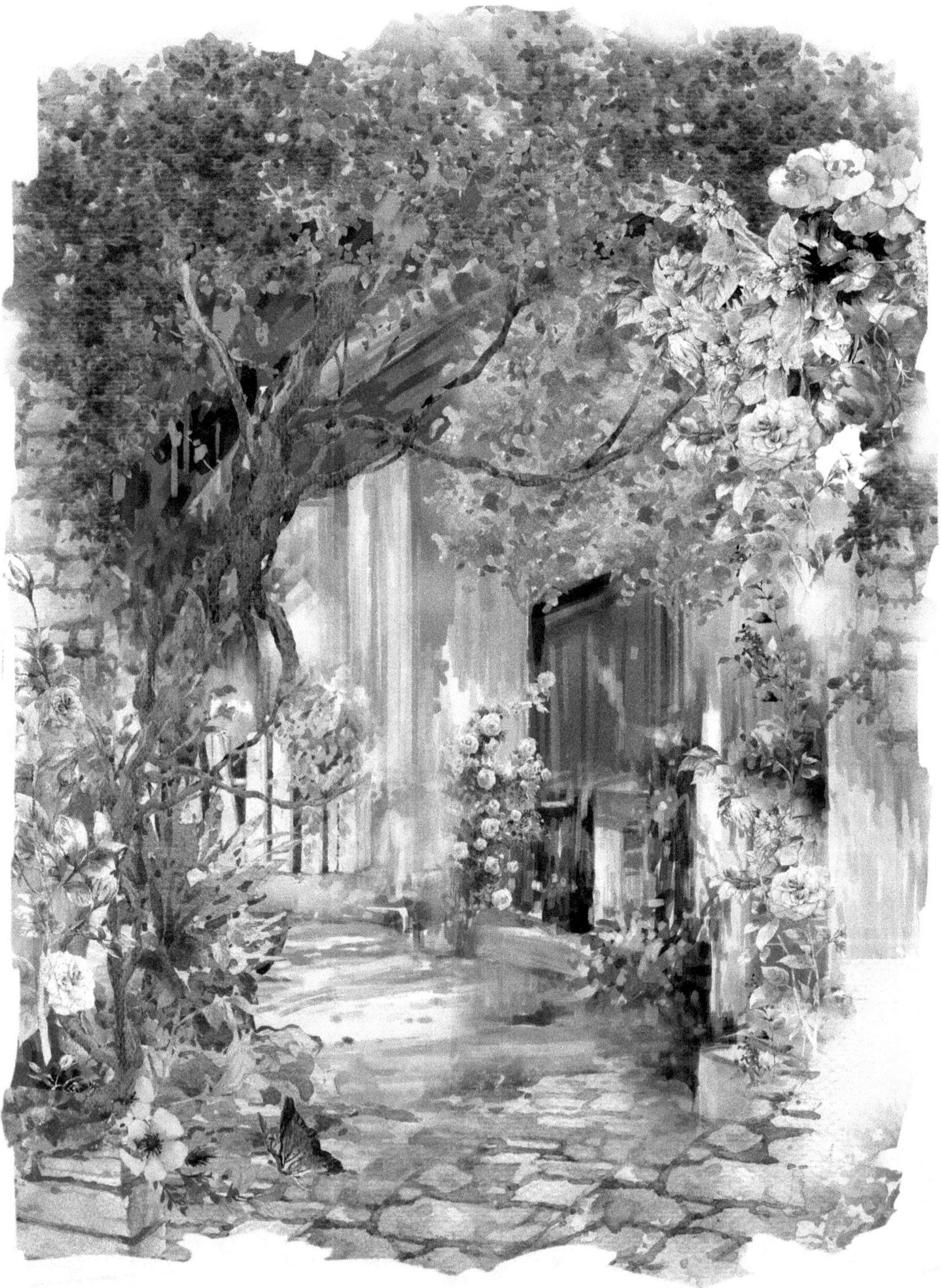

You have set me in a safe place

O LORD, YOU ARE MY PROTECTOR,
YOU ARE MY ROCK OF PROTECTION.
MY FORTRESS WHERE I WILL BE SAFE.

YOU ARE MY ROCK, MY FORTRESS,
HELP ME TO HONOR YOU AND BE LED BY YOU.
GIVE ME WISDOM AND DISCERNMENT TO SEE WHEN,
THE ENEMY HAS OR IS GOING TO SET A TRAP.
HELP ME TO BE QUICK TO FLEE AND OBEY YOUR VOICE OF INSTRUCTION
AND DIRECTION.

I ENTRUST MY SPIRIT INTO YOUR HANDS
THANK YOU FOR RESCUING ME AS YOU ARE A FAITHFUL GOD.
MY GOD IN WHOM I TRUST.

YOU HAVE SEEN ALL MY TROUBLES
AND YOU CARE ABOUT THE ANGUISH OF MY SOUL.
YOU HAVE NOT ALLOWED THE ENEMY TO SUCCEED
WITH ME OR MY LOVED ONES.
"YOU HAVE SET US IN A SAFE PLACE".
THANK YOU FOR PROTECTING ME AND MY LOVED ONES!
WE GIVE YOU GLORY AND PRAISE!
THANK YOU FOR YOUR PROVISIONS ALWAYS.

By: Maija The Poet.

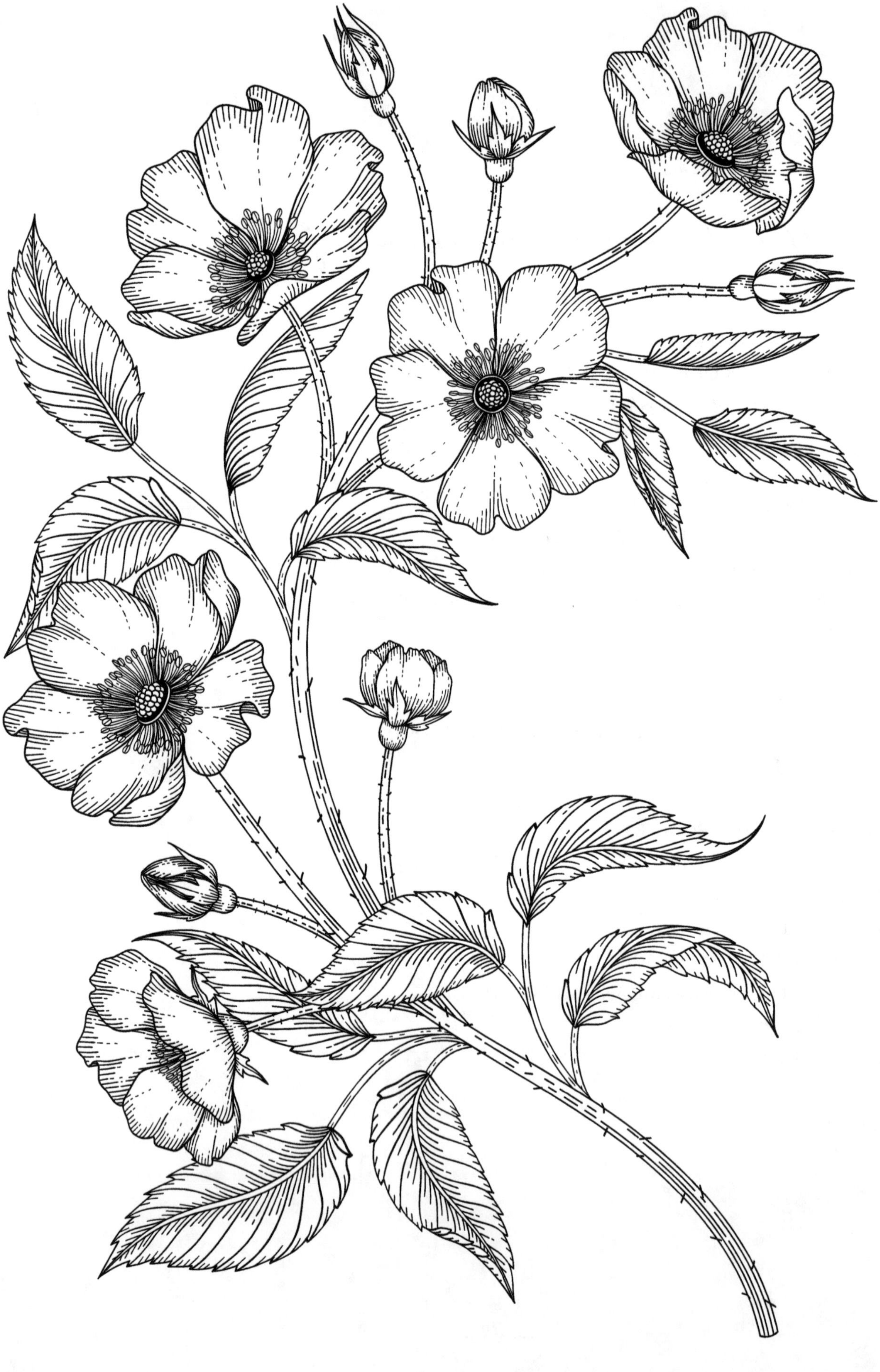

Fly my Child

WHO HAS STOPPED YOU MY CHILD FROM ACHIEVING ALL THAT I HAVE PLANNED FOR YOU? WHO HAS TIED YOU DOWN AND SAID.," **NO, WHO DO YOU THINK YOU ARE?"**
"HAVE YOU BELIEVED THE LIES THAT WERE TOLD TO YOU?" SAYING
"YOU WILL NEVER GO FAR!"

TURN TO ME AND MY WILL FOR YOU.
I HAVE CUT THE CORD; THE CHAIN IS GONE!
"LOOK AROUND NOW"," LIFT UP YOUR FEET"
"YOU ARE FREE." YOU HAVE BEEN SET FREE".
"COME FLY". COME FLY WITH ME!"
"FLY MY CHILD, "COME AND SEE."
THE PLANS I HAVE FOR THEE.
COME TO ME AND WE SHALL SEE.
THE PLANS I HAVE FOR THEE.
I CAN NOW HEAR YOU SAY.
"I CAN FLY" "I CAN FLY" "I AM FREE"
THANK YOU FOR SAVING ME!

By: Maija The Poet.
PRESS ON TOWARD THE GOAL
PHIL 3:8-14

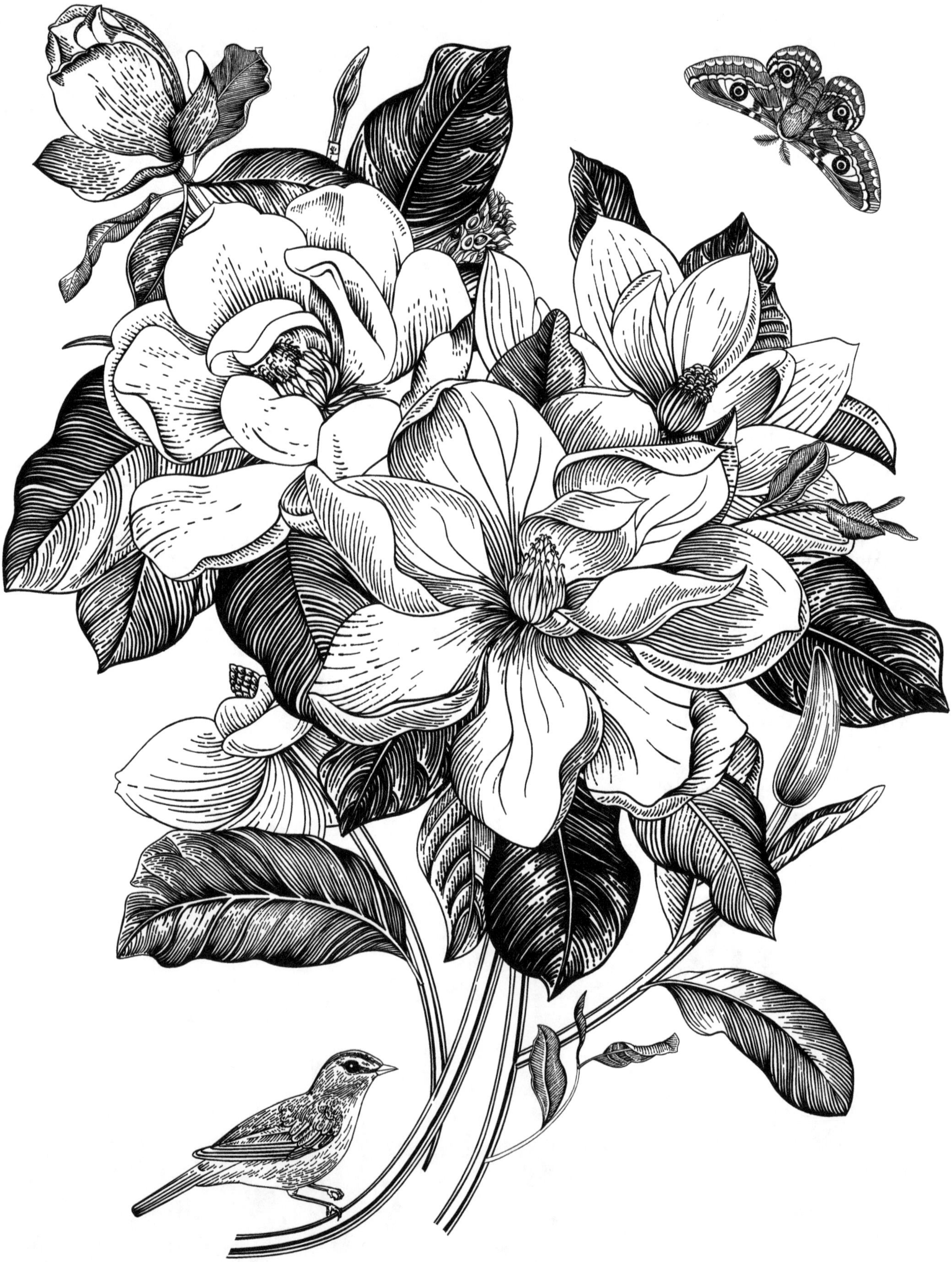

Even Me

WHY IS IT SO HARD TO SEE
THAT WE WERE CREATED BY HIM.
TO BE THE BEST THAT WE CAN BE.
WHY IS IT SO HARD TO SEE
THAT WE WERE CREATED FOR HIM
TO GIVE HIM WORSHIP AND GLORY
FOR ALL THE WORLD TO SEE
THAT HIS LOVE IS REAL
THAT HE PAID THE PRICE
FOR ALL TO SEE
THAT HE LOVES YOU AND ME.

7-22-1998

By Maija The Poet/ MJB/Mary Vincent-Babun

ALL THINGS WERE CREATED FOR HIM AND BY HIM.
COL. 1:1:16

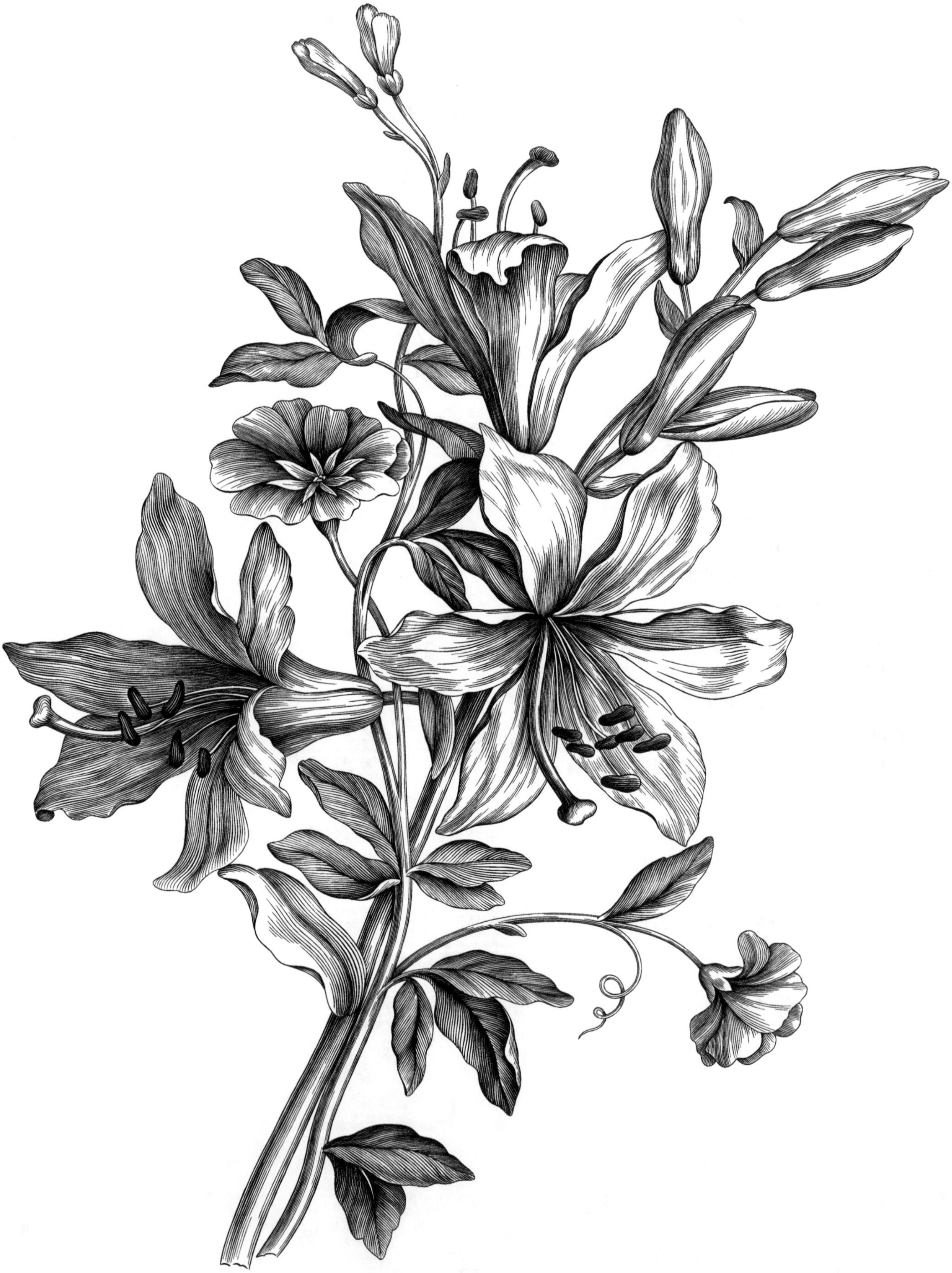

I have feet of clay

Oh, how I want to be used by Him,
but then I hesitate in the flesh and say "I think".

OH, HOW I WANT TO FOLLOW HIM TO THE FULLEST,
BUT THEN I SAY. "WILL I BE ABLE TO?"

I HAVE FEET OF CLAY, I'M IN THE POTTERS HAND,
I MAKE MISTAKES EVERYDAY; I DON'T HAVE ALL OF THE ANSWERS, JUST PRAISE!

By Maija The Poet/ MJB/Mary Vincent-Babun
Copyright

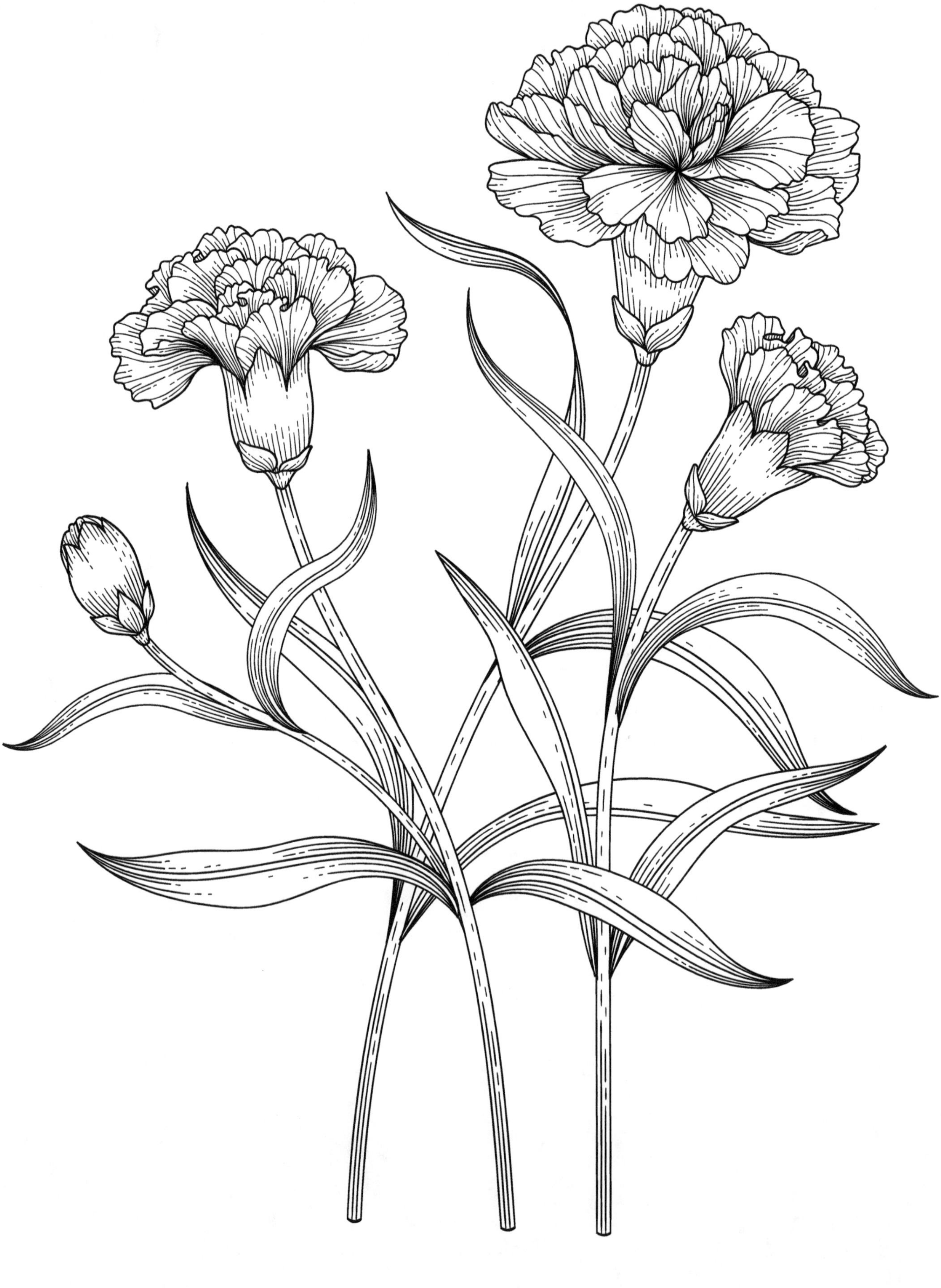

In Pain

DOES YOUR HEART HURT YOU?
IS YOUR MIND FULL OF THOUGHTS?
ARE YOU SEEKING SOLACE TOO?

IS YOUR MIND FULL OF SHOULDS AND OUGHTS?
DO YOU PICK UP THE PAPER AND TO YOUR DISMAY
THERE ARE SADIST AND TERRIBLE COMMENTARIES TODAY.
EVERYWHERE YOU LOOK, YOU SEE VIOLENCE, CRUELTY AND SO MUCH PAIN,
WHAT ARE WE AS A PEOPLE TO GAIN?

OUR FAMILIES ARE MISSING OUT OF VALUABLE TIME.
TIME TOGETHER IS, OH SO RARE.
EVERYBODY IS SCURRYING WITH SCHEDULES AND FRIENDS.
THEY DON'T SEEM TO BE AWARE.

By Maija The Poet/ MJB/Mary Vincent-Babun

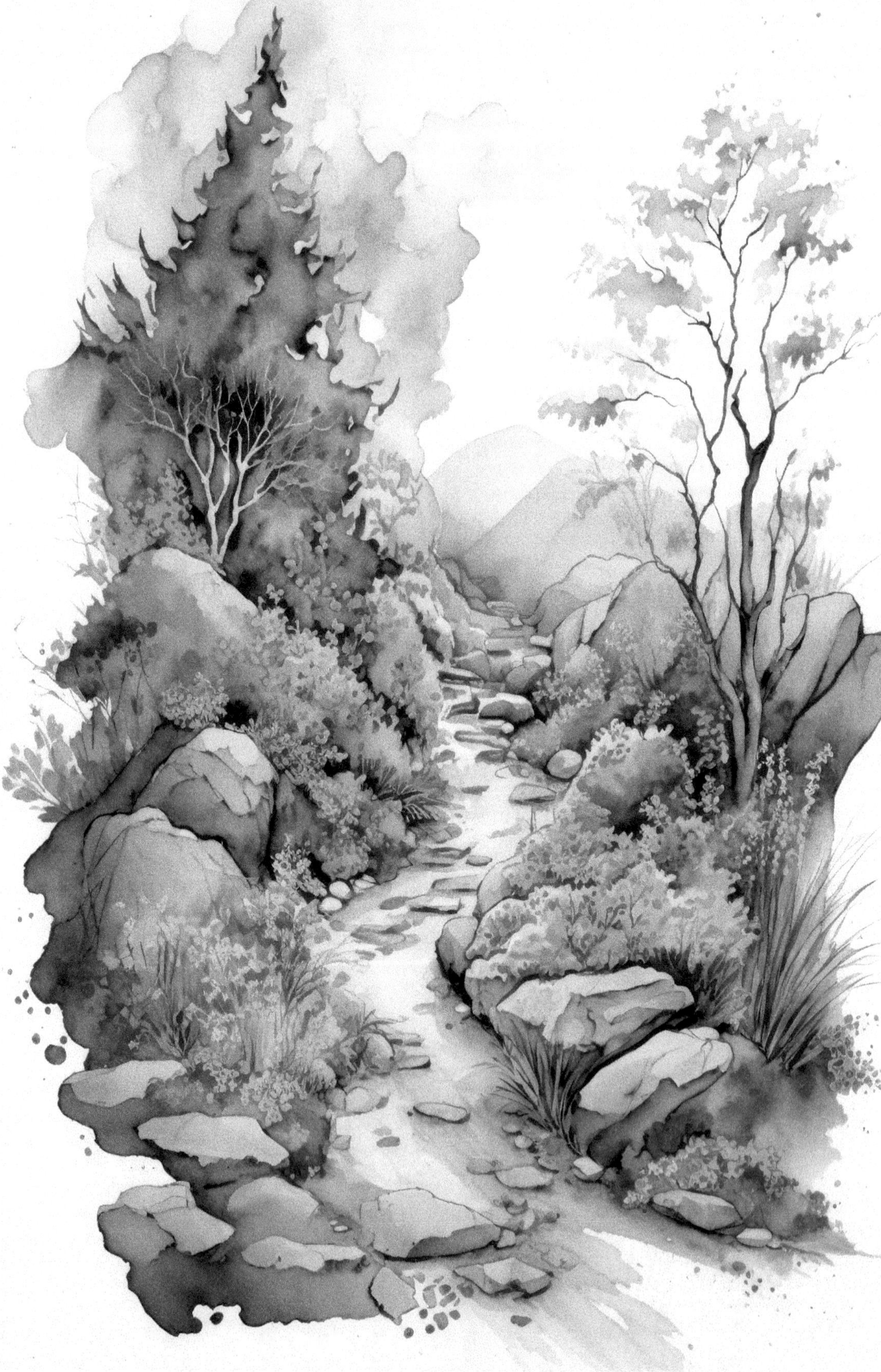

It is not me, but God

IT IS NOT ME, BUT GOD WHO WILLS AND WORKS THROUGH ME.

IT IS GOD WHO SHOWS ME WHERE TO GO AND WHOM TO REACH.
I SUBMIT TO GODS LEADERSHIP AND GIVE MYSELF TO HIS PURPOSES.
JAMES 4:6 "GOD OPPOSES THE PROUD BUT GIVES GRACE TO THE HUMBLE."
BUILT BY GODS HANDS, NOT MANS. MAY I BE OBEDIENT TO HIS CALLING.

MAY I BE SALT AND LIGHT TO OTHERS
SO THEY MAY COME CLOSE TO YOU JESUS!
PLEASE FORM YOUR CHARACTER IN ME. TRANSFORM ME LORD!
THANK YOU FOR YOUR GIFT OF THE HOLY SPIRIT OF GOD.

I SURRENDER TO THE CONTROL OF THE HOLY SPIRIT, WHERE I WILL EXPERIENCE FREEDOM
FROM THE CONTROL OF SIN AND THE FLESH. ROM 8

SPIRIT OF GOD, "I SURRENDER TO YOU".
I AM SEALED WITH THE HOLY SPIRIT.
I AM INDWELT BY GODS OWN SPIRIT! THANK YOU LORD
"YOU WILL RECEIVE POWER WHEN THE HOLY SPIRIT COMES ON YOU". ACTS 1:8

I AM AN ADOPTED CHILD OF GOD. ROM. 8:17

"NOW IF WE ARE CHILDREN, THEN WE ARE HEIRS, HEIRS OF GOD AND CO-HEIRS WITH CHRIST.
DIVINE GRACE- "TO DIE IS GAIN" PHIL 1:21

"I CONSIDER THAT OUR PRESENT SUFFERINGS ARE NOT WORTH COMPARING WITH THE GLORY
THAT WILL BE REVEALED IN US. ROM. 8:18

By Maija The Poet/ MJB/Mary Vincent-Babun
7-1-14

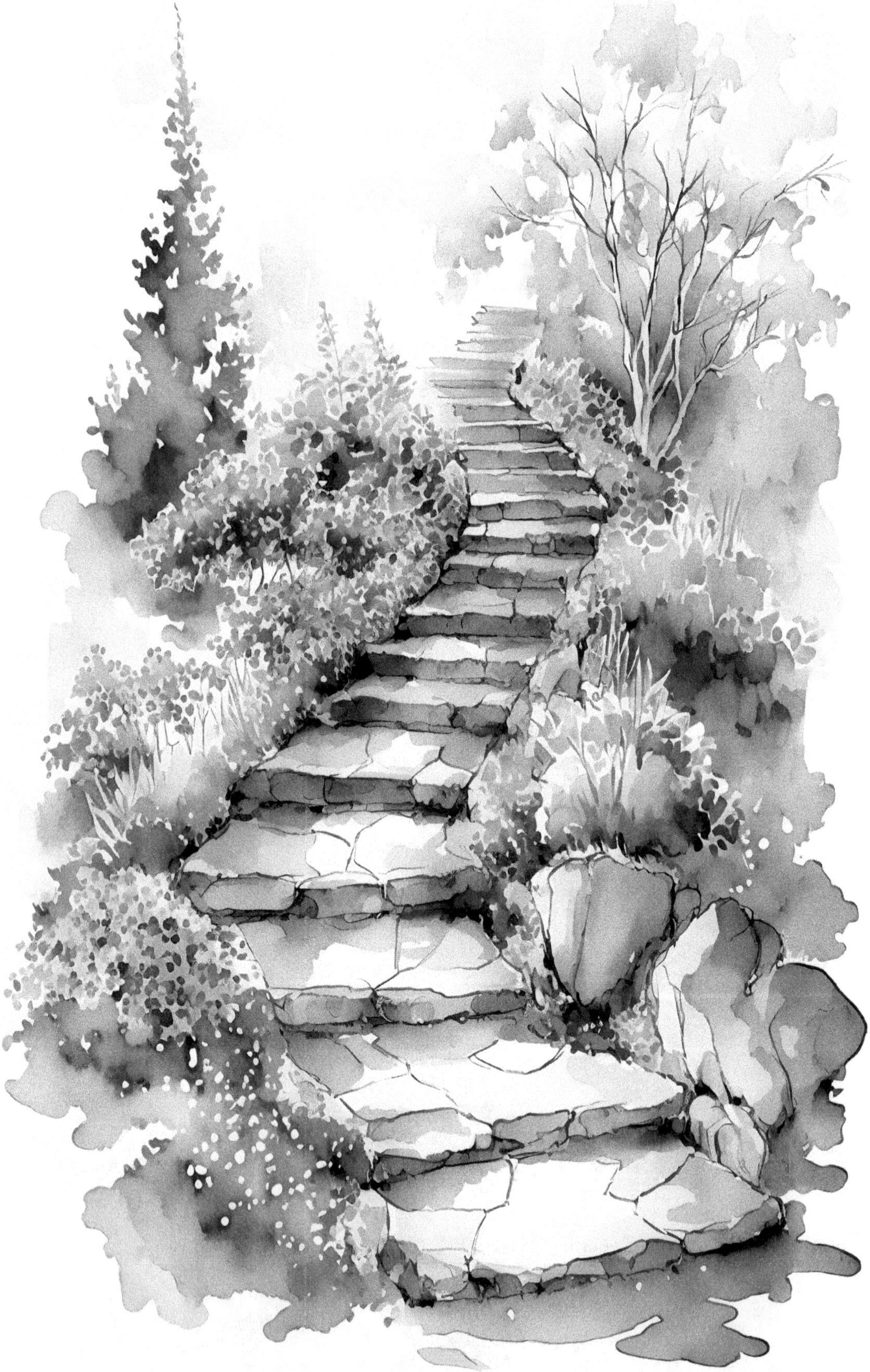

Listen to your Tears

LISTEN, LISTEN TO YOUR TEARS
DON'T SUBMERGE YOUR THOUGHTS OR YOUR FEARS.
IT IS THROUGH LISTENING THAT YOU WILL UNDERSTAND
THE RHYME AND REASON OF THE MASTER'S HAND.

WHEN YOU CAN IDENTIFY THE FEELING WITH THE EMOTION
YOU CAN BE HEALED AND MOVE ON BEYOND RECOGNITION.
BECAUSE YOU WILL BE FREE TO LOVE, FREE TO MOVE, FREE TO MAKE BETTER CHOICES.
AND WHEN YOU DO MAKE THE RIGHT CHOICES FOR YOU,
YOUR HEART WILL REJOICE AND YOU WILL TO.

SO DON'T HIDE YOUR HEAD, WHEN YOU FEEL THE STING OF TEARS
JUST REMEMBER TO TELL YOURSELF
"WAIT, I MUST LISTEN TO MY TEARS."
I'M ALIVE AND LISTENING, NO LONGER IN FEAR.
SO THANK YOU LORD FOR HEALING TEARS
THANK YOU FOR BEING WITH ME ALL OF THESE YEARS.
NOW, MAYBE I CAN HELP MY PEERS.
BE BLESSED. LISTEN TO YOUR TEARS.

By Maija The Poet/ MJB/Mary Vincent-Babun
Copyright
1/30/2014

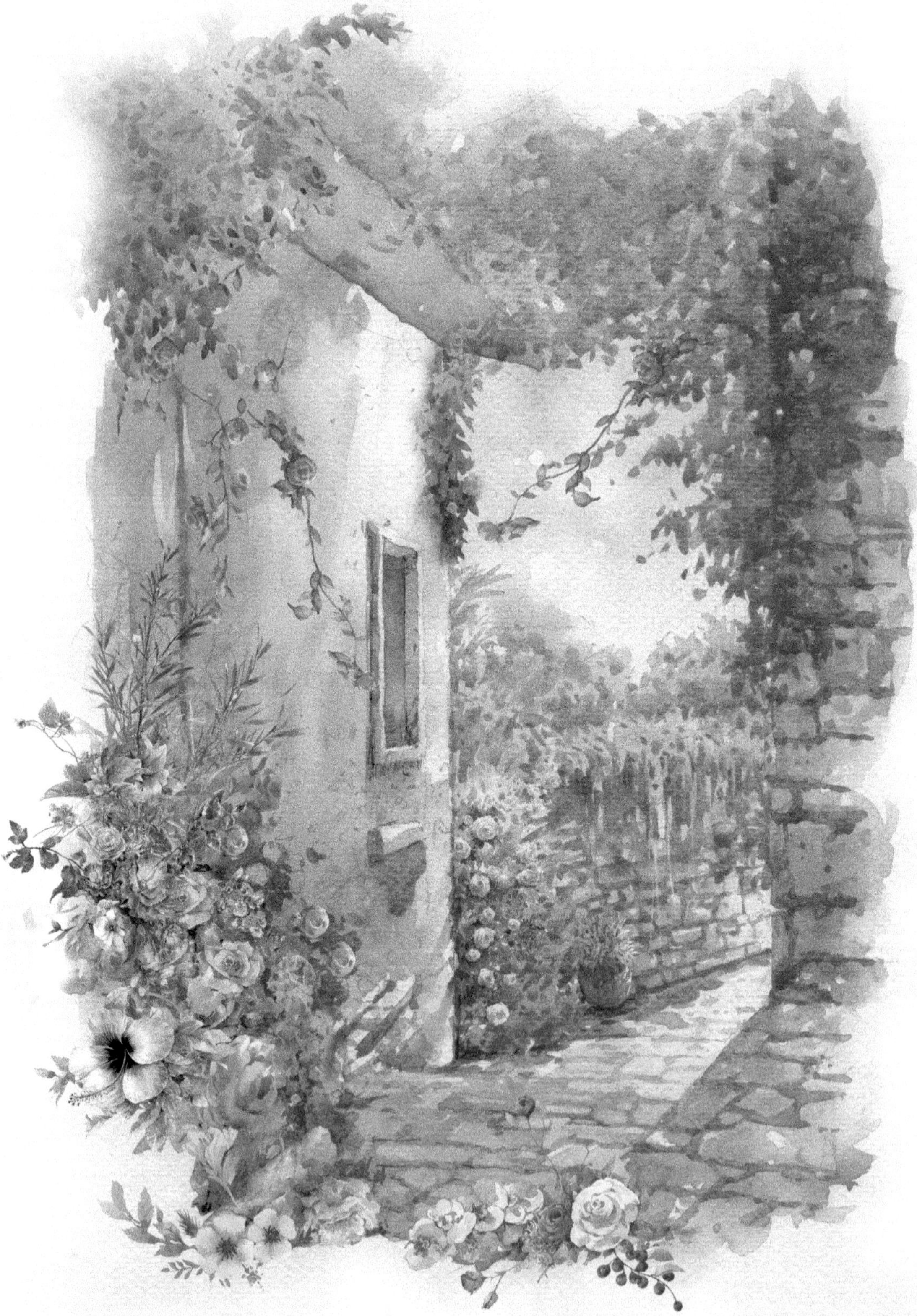

Mother

M IS FOR MOTHER, ONE OF ITS' KIND

O IS FOR ONE, THE ONLY ONE FOR ME.

T IS FOR TENDER, THE MOMENTS THAT WE SHARED

H IS FOR HUG, YOU'D OFTEN GIVE TO ME

E IS ETERNITY, I'LL ALWAYS LOVE YOU

R IS FOR RESTFUL, YOUR LIFE MAY IT BE.

I COULDN'T FIND A CARD, SO I DECIDED TO MAKE MY OWN.
I HOPE AND KNOW YOU HAD A BEAUTIFUL BIRTHDAY.
BIRTHDAYS ARE SO SPECIAL
THE MEMORY'S OLD AND THE NEW
I HOPE THIS YEAR WILL BE BETTER THAN EVER BEFORE.

H IS FOR HAPPY, YOU HAVE MADE ME.
A IS FOR ALWAYS BEING YOU.
P IS FOR PARENT, WHICH YOU HAVE BEEN
P IS FOR PENNY, WHICH WE REALLY NEEDED TO SAVE.
Y IS FOR YEARLY, THIS BIRTHDAY OF YOURS.

B IS FOR BEAUTIFUL, THE MOM THAT YOU ARE
I IS FOR INTENSE, HOW SERIOUS YOU CAN BE
R IS FOR REARING, SOMETHING YOU DID FOR US ALL.
T IS FOR THANK-YOU, WE LOVE YOU DEARLY FOR BEING OUR MOM
H IS FOR HEART, WHICH YOU DO HAVE
D IS FOR DEARLY, I HOLD YOU CLOSE TO ME
A IS FOR APPLE, WHICH YOU REALLY LIKED TO EAT.
Y IS FOR YES, HAVE A VERY HAPPY, HAPPY BIRTHDAY.

MOTHER, HAPPY BIRTHDAY TO YOU.

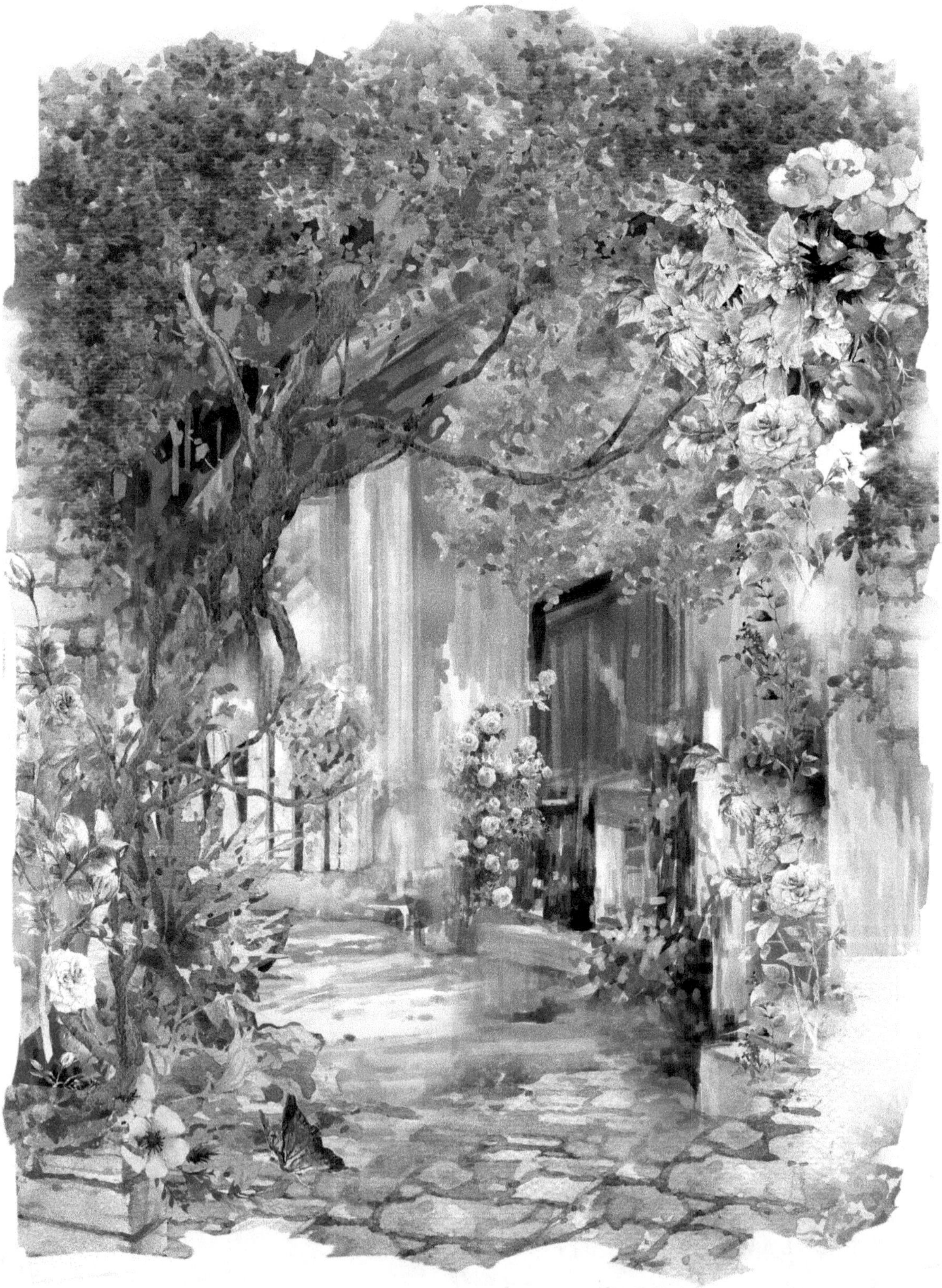

On going Problems?

ARE YOU PLAGUED BY A PERSISTENT PROBLEM?
LIKE A DRIPPING FAUCET, MONEY, CHILDREN, ILLNESS.
THERE SEEMS TO BE SO MANY OF THEM.

YOU'RE MIND FLITTERS HERE, YOUR MIND FLITTERS THERE.
WHOM DO I TALK TO, DOES ANYONE CARE?
ALL SEEM TO BE CONSUMED WITH PROBLEMS OF THEIR OWN.
ARE WE ALL RUNNING IN CIRCLES, LIKE LEAVES THAT ARE WIND BLOWN?

FLYING HERE, FLYING THERE, FLOATING HERE, AND FLOATING THERE.
WHEN I FINALLY REACH MY DESTINY.
CAN I REST MY MIND WHILE SITTING IN A CHAIR?
AS I SIT UPON MY CHAIR, I CATCH THE BREEZE AND THE REFRESHING AIR.
I BREATHE IN AND OUT AND FEEL THE PRESSURES LEAVE.
AS I SIT BACK AND RELAX IN MY CHAIR.
LIFE ISN'T ALWAYS OR SEEMS TO BE FAIR,
SO I MUST TRUST AND KNOW THAT, SOME WAY,
SOMEHOW I WILL GET OUT OF THIS NIGHTMARE.
MAYBE IT'S MY MIND THAT ISN'T THINKING RIGHT.
WHAT HAVE I BEEN THINKING THAT IS MAKING ME SO UP TIGHT?
CHANGE YOUR THOUGHTS AND YOU CHANGE YOUR BEHAVIOR.
BECAUSE THOUGHTS CREATE ACTIONS, YOU GO FIGURE.
SO IF I SEETHE PROBLEM IN A DIFFERENT WAY.
IF I SEE IT AS AN OPPORTUNITY TO SAY.
YOU HAVE GOTTEN MY ATTENTION,
SO I WILL STOP, LOOK, AND LISTEN.

IF THE SINK IS LEAKING, I WILL CALL A PLUMBER,
IF I AM STRESSED OUT, I JUST NEED TO SLUMBER.
IF FINANCES ARE A CONSTANT THREAT,
THEN I MUST DO SOMETHING ABOUT IT AND NOT JUST FRET.
SO CHANGE YOUR THOUGHTS AND YOUR ACTIONS TOO.
YOU WILL SOLVE YOUR PROBLEMS AND YOU'LL KNOW WHAT TO DO.
STOP, LOOK, AND LISTEN, WHAT DO YOU HEAR,
THE ANSWERS ARE WITHIN YOU. HAPPY NEW YEAR…..

Dec 18, 20113
By: Maija The Poet.

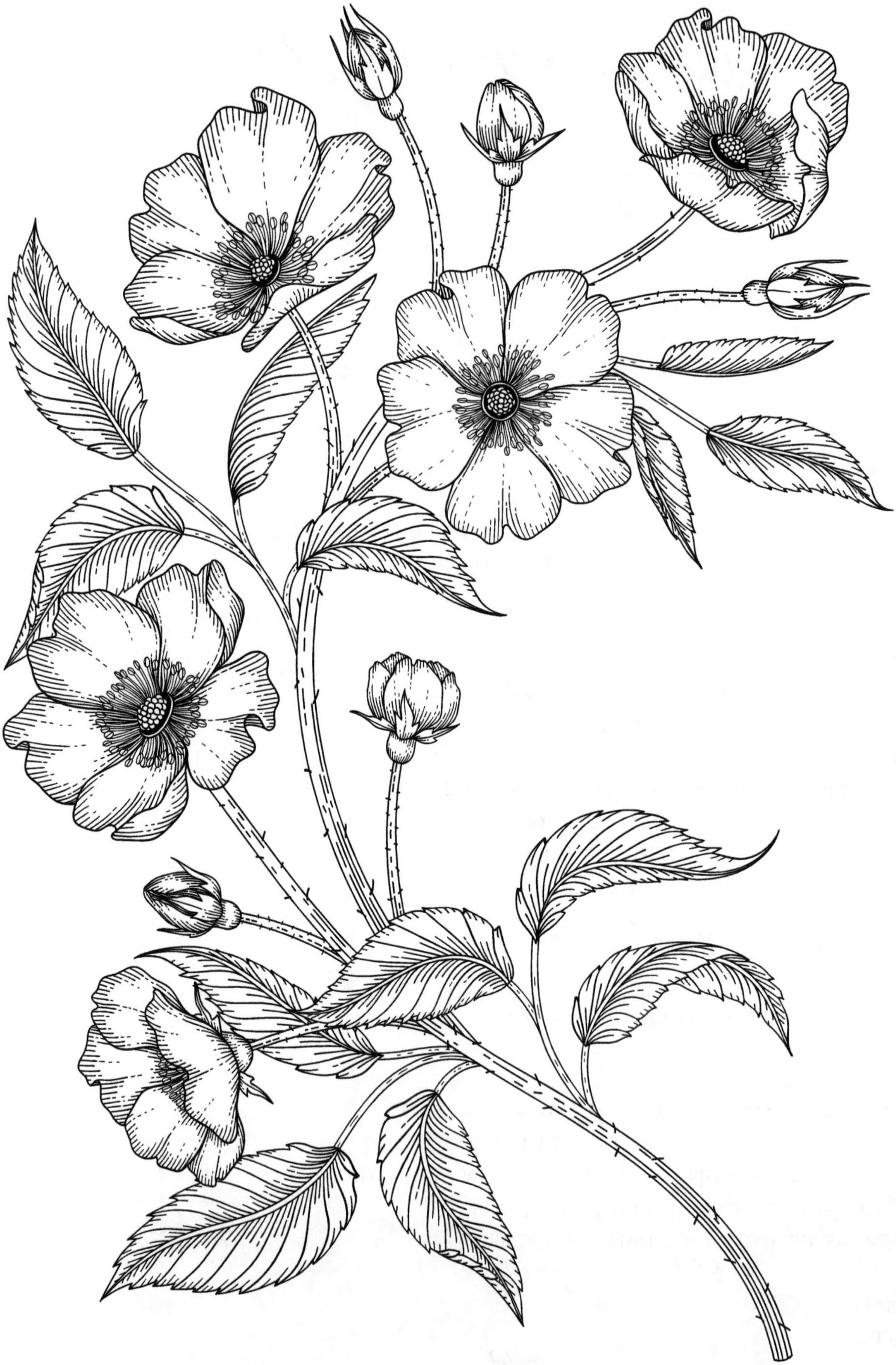

Running Away

HAVE YOU EVER FELT LIKE RUNNING AWAY?

FROM YOUR FAMILY, FROM YOUR RESPONSIBILITY, FROM YOUR KIDS.

FROM EVERYTHING AND EVERYONE?

BUT RUNNING TO A PLACE OF QUIET, REST, RETREAT, SLEEP

I FOUND MYSELF RUNNING AWAY FROM HOME WHEN I WAS 17

TRYING TO FIND LOVE

THEN WHEN I WAS IN MY 20'S I FOUND CHRIST AS MY LORD AND SAVIOUR.

HE LOVED ME TO HIMSELF.

I FELT SO GOOD, SO CLEAN, AND SO PURE, SO CLOSE TO GOD.

THEN WHEN I WAS IN MY 50'S,

I CAUGHT MYSELF RUNNING AGAIN.

TOO MUCH RESPONSIBILITY

TOO MUCH PAIN

TOO MANY DEMANDS

SO, I LEFT FOR AWHILE VISITING FAMILY AND SEEING OTHER COUNTRIES

I WAS ON A JOURNEY

I MET PEOPLE WHO LOVED THE LORD AND I MET PEOPLE WHO DID NOT WANT TO HEAR,

LET ALONE KNOW THE LORD. I MET REALLY GREAT PEOPLE WHO JUST SAID.

"I'M NOT RELIGIOUS".

By Maija The Poet

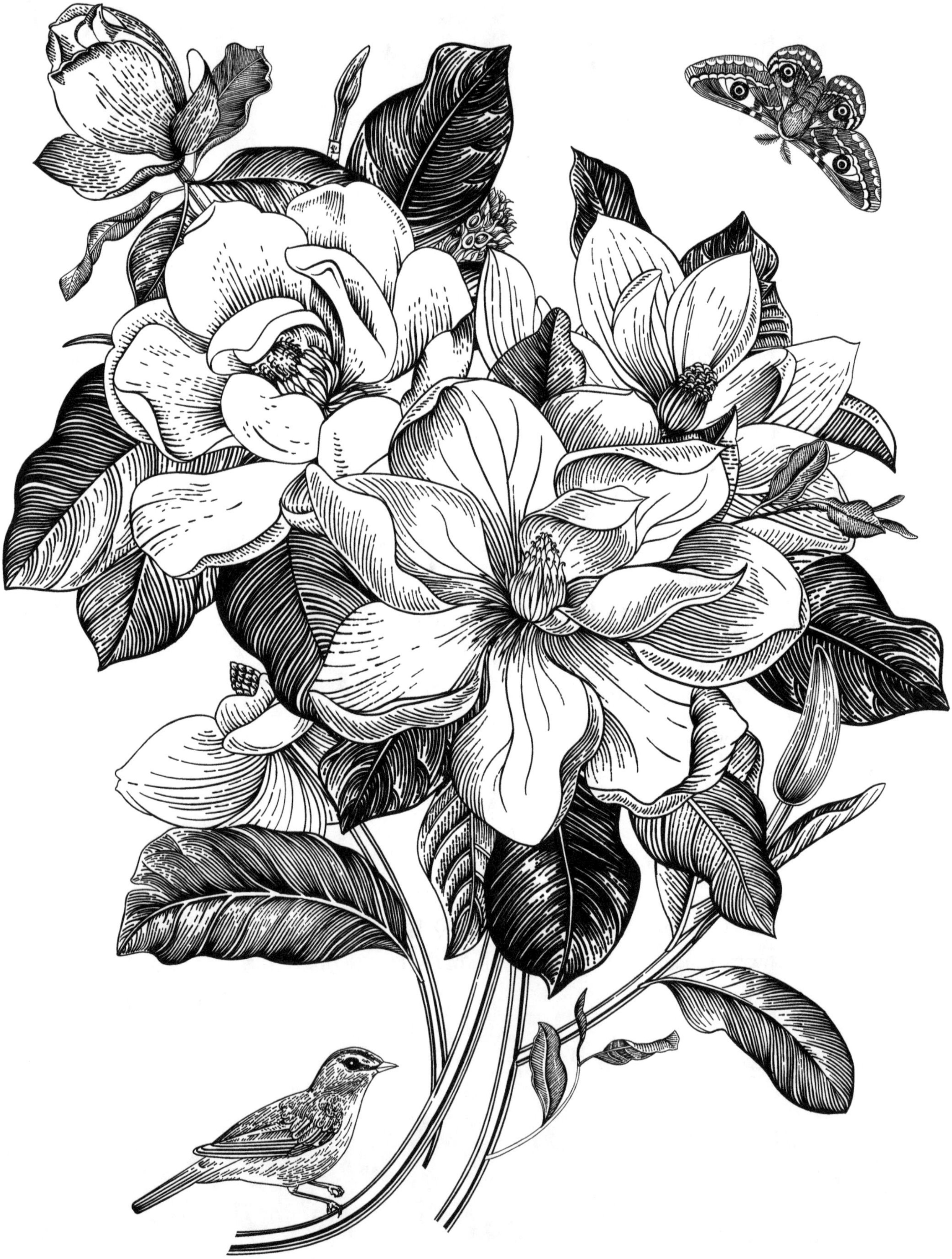

Thank You Glady

THANK YOU GLADYS FOR THE EXAMPLE YOU HAVE BEEN.
BEING QUIET IN THE BACKGROUND BUT DEFINITELY GETTING THINGS DONE.
YOU'RE EXAMPLE AS A HARD WORKING WOMAN
IN THE HOME, IN THE MARKET PLACE, AND WHEREVER YOU CAN
HAS BEEN NOTICED BY FAMILY AND FRIENDS AND MANY OUT THERE.

YOU TAKE TIME TO TAKE CARE OF YOU, AND FIX YOUR HAIR.
BUT THE GREATEST EXAMPLE IS YOUR HONESTY WITH ALL.
YOU'RE LOVE TO YOUR HUSBAND SONNY AND BACKBONE TO LEAN ON
THAT MADE HIM FEEL SO HAPPY AND HE SURE FELT TALL.
TO HAVE YOU BY HIS SIDE, WITH YOUR CHILDREN IN TOW.
YOU BOTH ARE ADMIRED AND APPRECIATED SO.
SO PLEASE DON'T THINK THAT NO ONE CAN SEE.
THE MOST WONDERFUL EXAMPLE AS A WOMAN,
A WIFE, A MOTHER AND GRANDMOTHER COULD BE.
THANK YOU FOR SHOWING ALL OF US THIS AMAZING PATH.
TO BE A GODLY WOMAN AND OH WHAT A TASK.

Maija/MJB/Mary Vincent Babun/
Copyright 2014
To Connie Bushes Mother

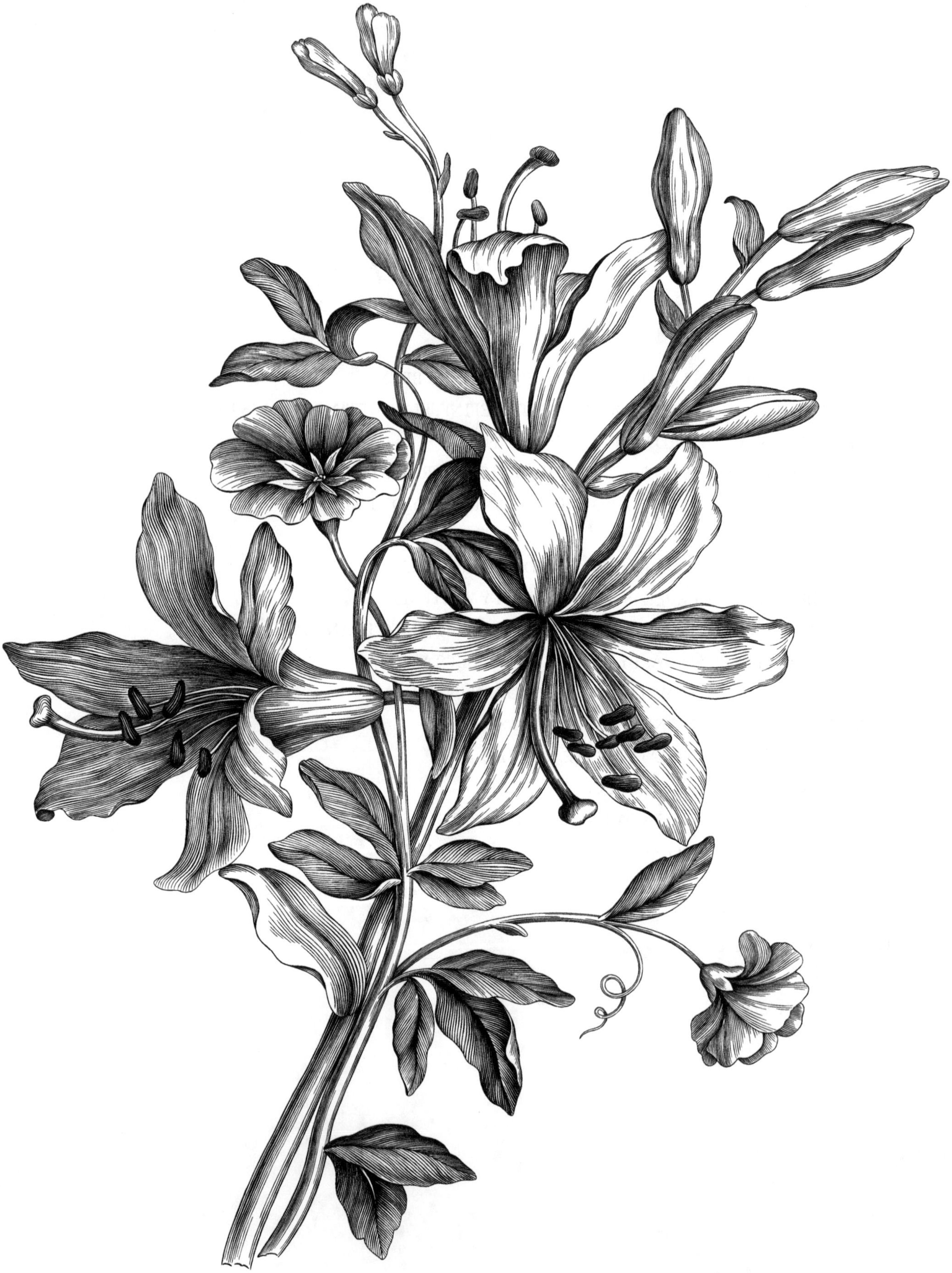

The Masters' Touch

I SING FOR JOY, AS I LOOK BACK AT ALL THE YEARS' I'VE LIVED,
I SEE THAT FROM THE BEGINNING, UP TO THIS VERY MOMENT.
I HAVE BEEN TOUCHED BY THE MASTERS' HAND.

I SING FOR JOY, AS HE CREATED ME IN MY MOTHERS' WOMB,
AND WILL BE WITH ME UNTIL THEY LAY THIS BODY IN THE TOMB.
THE BODY THAT I WAS GIVEN WHILE HERE ON THIS EARTH
WILL BE RAISED WITH HIM ON THAT RESURRECTION DAY BIRTH.

I SING FOR JOY, AS HE TOUCHED ME ON QUINCY, THE MAGNIFICENT U.P., UPON THE HILL
HE NEVER FORGOT ME; HE WAS ALWAYS BESIDE ME, GENTLE AND STILL.
HAS BEEN TRAVELING WITH ME, FROM STATE TO STATE,
HELPING ME ALWAYS WITH MY MATE.

I SING FOR JOY, AS HE'S WALKED WITH ME THROUGH THE SNOW DRIVEN STORMS.
HE'S SAT BESIDE ME AS A TEEN ON THE ROCK WHERE I WAS BORN.
LOOKING UP, THE CLOUDS WERE SO MAGNIFICENT IN FORM.
WE CHATTED FOR HOURS AS MY HEART WAS TORN.

I SING FOR JOY, AS HE ASSURED ME OF HIS PRESENCE FROM THE BEGINNING TO THE END.
IT WAS HIS WORK I'D BE DOING ALONG THE WAY.
HE WOULD SEND PEOPLE TO ME AND WE WOULD BECOME FRIENDS.
I JUST NEEDED TO BE ATTENTIVE, TO LISTEN AND OBEY.
NOW THE YEARS HAVE PASSED, AND MY MOUTH MUST PROCLAIM,
THIS TRULY WAS TO BE GOD'S AIM.
TO HAVE HIS LOVE WITH ME IN THE MORNING AND HIS FAITHFULNESS AT NIGHT.
HE CERTAINLY HAS MADE EVERYTHING ALL RIGHT.

I SING FOR JOY AT THE WORKS OF HIS HANDS
FOR THE MULTITUDE OF PEOPLE I'VE MET, JUST LIKE THE SAND.
I SING FOR JOY, FOR HE HAS MADE ME GLAD, HIS LOVE FOR ME AND ALL, IS SO MUCH.
I SING FOR JOY, AS I PRAISE THE LORD
FOR HIM, FOR
THE MASTERS TOUCH.

10-18-98

Maija/MJB/Vincent Babun

Psalm 92:4 "YOU HAVE DONE SO MUCH FOR ME, O LORD. NO WONDER I AM GLAD! I SING FOR JOY."

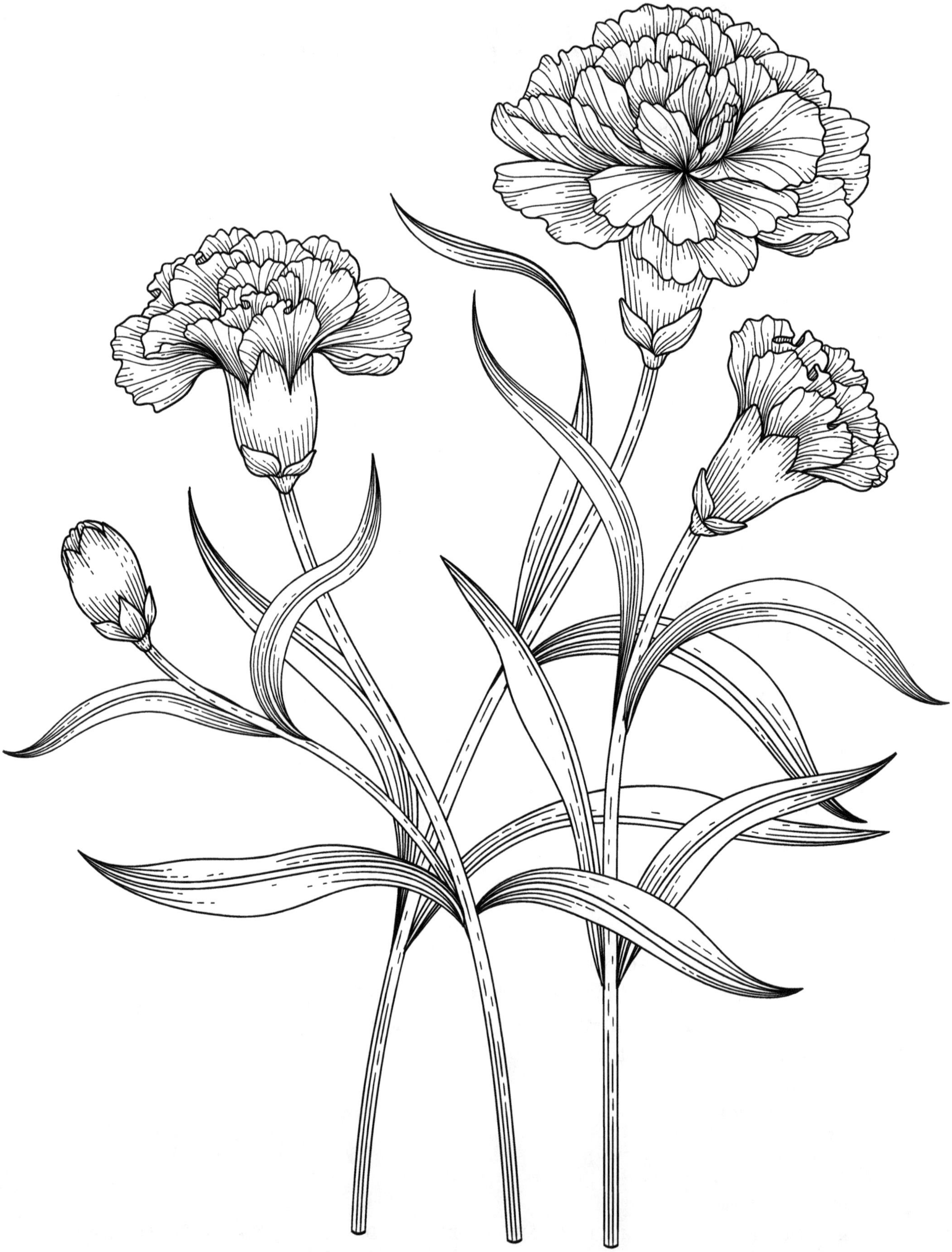

Today

THEREFORE GOD AGAIN SET A CERTAIN DAY, CALLING IT TODAY. HEBREWS 4:7A

LORD, AS I HEAR YOUR VOICE TODAY,
PLEASE HELP ME TO LISTEN AND OBEY.
GIVE ME THE SELF DISCIPLINE THAT I NEED.
TO GO ON AND HEAR AND HEED.
HEED YOUR COUNSEL AND MY EYES OPENED WIDE,
TO THE SCRIPTURES BY FAITH, WITH YOU BY MY SIDE.
ALLOW ME TO ENTER IN, INTO YOUR REST.
WITH YOU AT THE CENTER TO TEACH ME YOUR BEST.
I LOVE YOU MY LORD, SOFTEN MY HEART.
QUICKEN MY SPIRIT, TO ENTER…NOT DART.
LORD, AS I HEAR YOUR VOICE TODAY,
PLEASE HELP ME TO LISTEN AND TO OBEY.

Written By: Maija The Poet/MJB/Vincent-Babun
Copyright: 6-11-1986

THEREFORE GOD AGAIN SET A CERTAIN DAY, CALLING IT TODAY, WHEN A LONG TIME LATER HE SPOKE THROUGH DAVID, AS WAS SAID BEFORE:
"TODAY, IF YOU HEAR HIS VOICE, DO NOT HARDEN YOUR HEARTS." HEBREWS 4:7

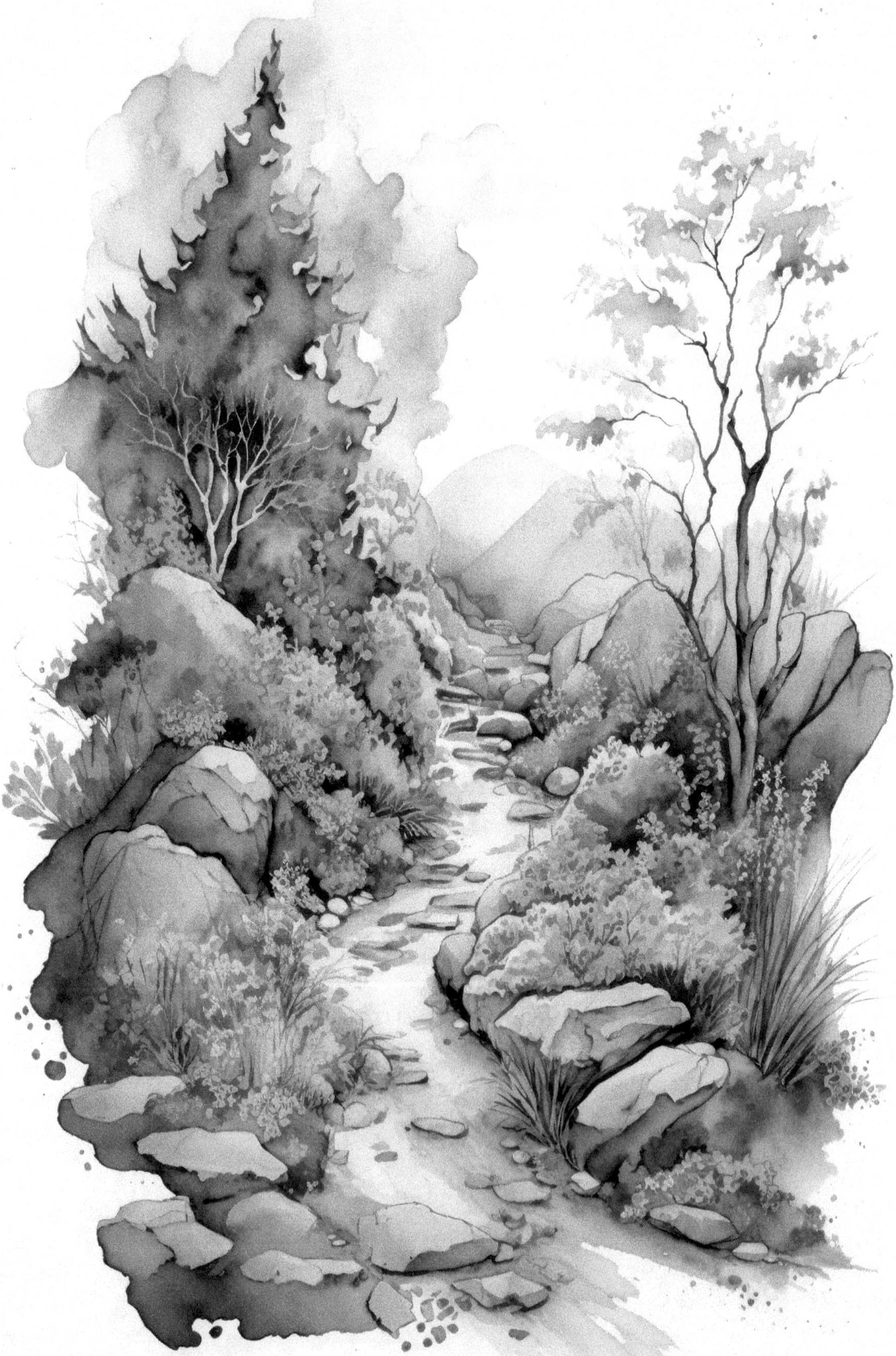

Welcome Back

THE LEAVES ARE FALLING ONE BY ONE
VERY SOON, SUMMER WILL BE GONE.
THE BUSSES WILL BE GASSED AND OILED,
AND READY FOR THE ROAD.

THE BUS DRIVERS WATCH EACH LITTLE GIRL AND BOY
AS THE BUSSES UNLOAD
THE CHILDREN WITH THEIR BACKPACKS ON
STEPPING OFF THE BUSSES, THEY RUN HITHER AND YON.

EACH ONE GREETING THEIR FRIENDS FROM LAST YEAR
HUGGING AND HIGH FIVING, ALL IN GOOD CHEER
ALL OF THEM HEAD FOR THE OPENED SCHOOL DOOR
TO WELCOME THEM INTO THE SCHOOL ONCE MORE.

Copyright: Maija/MJB/Mary Vincent/Babun
7-28-14

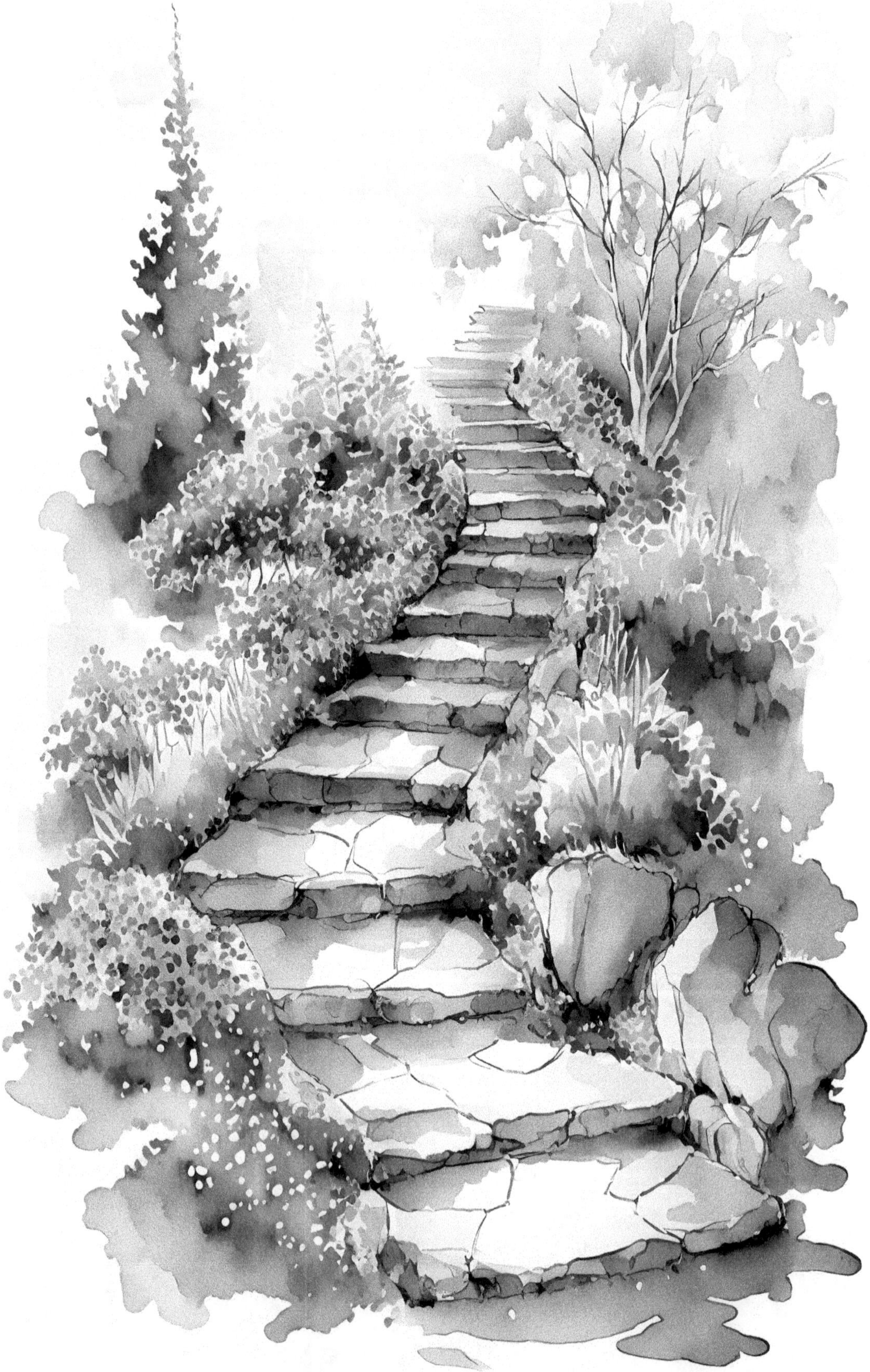

Fear God: By Maija The Poet

HOW DOES ONE KNOW WHO TO VOTE FOR?
IT IS QUITE EASY AS YOU WILL SEE.
THE UNGODLY TAX YOU ABOVE AND BEYOND.
NOT TAX FREE,
THEY DRINK AND EAT AND DEMAND YOU PAY.

THEY ARE INSPIRED WITH A MONTHLY WAGE AND EAT FOOD EVERY DAY.
THEY REQUIRE YOU TO PAY FOR THE INFIDELS IN THE LAND.
THEY RECEIVE BONUSES AND PENSIONS, THAT IS THEIR DEMAND.
WHILE YOU WORK HARD AND TRY TO MAKE DO.
THEY LIVE IN SECURE HOMES WITH SECURITY GUARDS ALL AROUND.
WHILE WE TRY TO GET HOME SAFELY.
WHILE THE RIOTS ABOUND.
DO THEY FEAR GOD? I DON'T THINK SO.
WHAT DOES FEAR GOD MEAN?
LET'S GIVE IT AGO.

THEY WHOM FEAR GOD, THINK OF ALL PEOPLE, NOT A SELECT FEW.
ALL PEOPLE ARE MADE EQUAL, AND THEY PROVIDE JOBS AND HELP THEM TO
STAND UP ON THEIR OWN TWO FEET TO.
THEY STAND FOR GODLY VIRTUES LIKE,
DO UNTO OTHERS AS YOU WOULD HAVE THEM DO UNTO YOU.
WHOM WILL YOU VOTE FOR?
THE GODLESS ONES, OR THOSE WHO FEAR GOD.
ONE WILL SHOW RANCOR, THE OTHERS RESTORE.
SO, TELL ME, WHO WILL YOU VOTE FOR?

By Maija The Poet

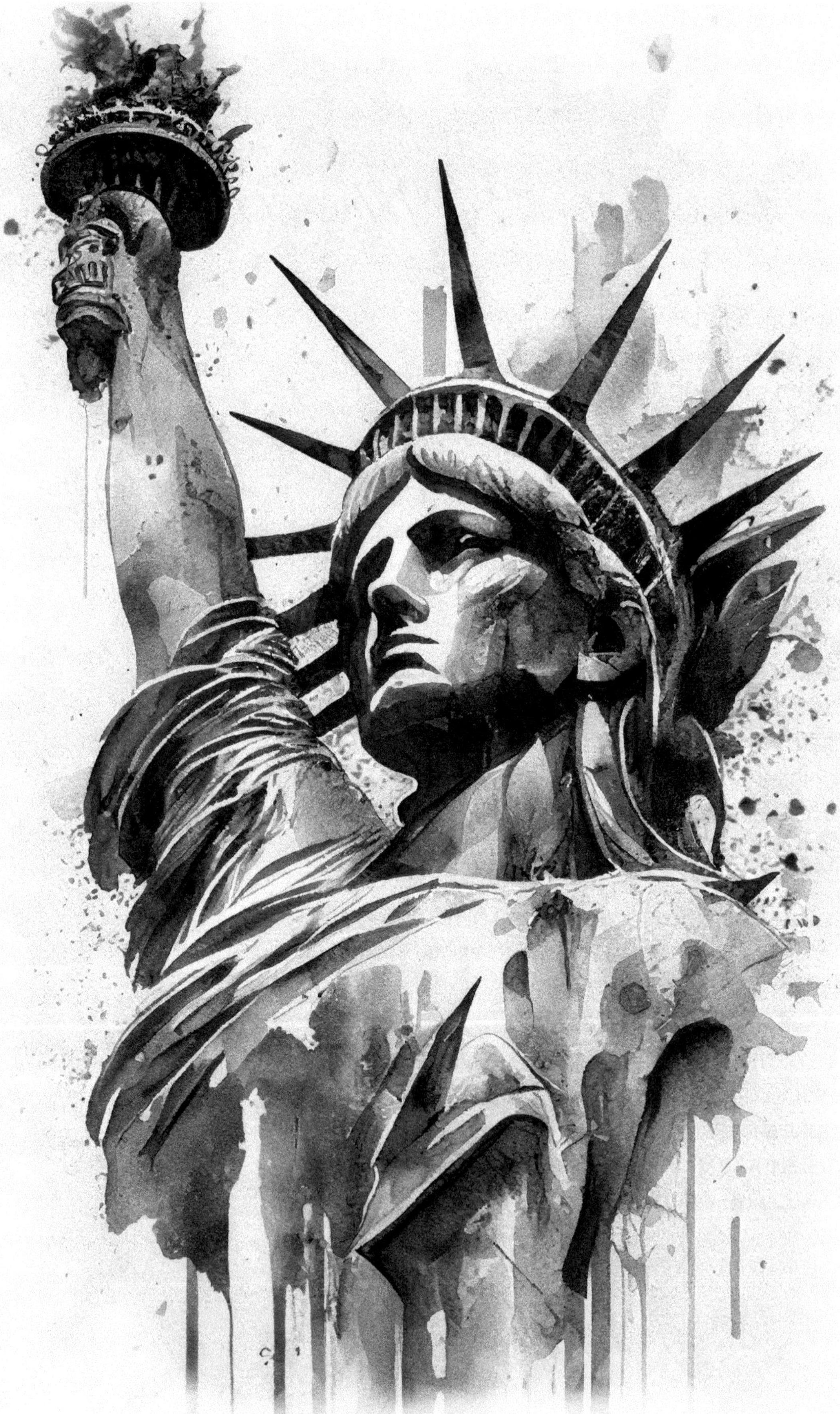

United We Stand

For united we stand, divided we fall
And if we are all together
We shall all stand tall
Let no one cause us
To split and fall
Because we are one nation
Under God, indivisible and justice for all
So, stand tall, don't fall
For the visible and invisible enemies
Will destroy us all.

By Maija The Poet

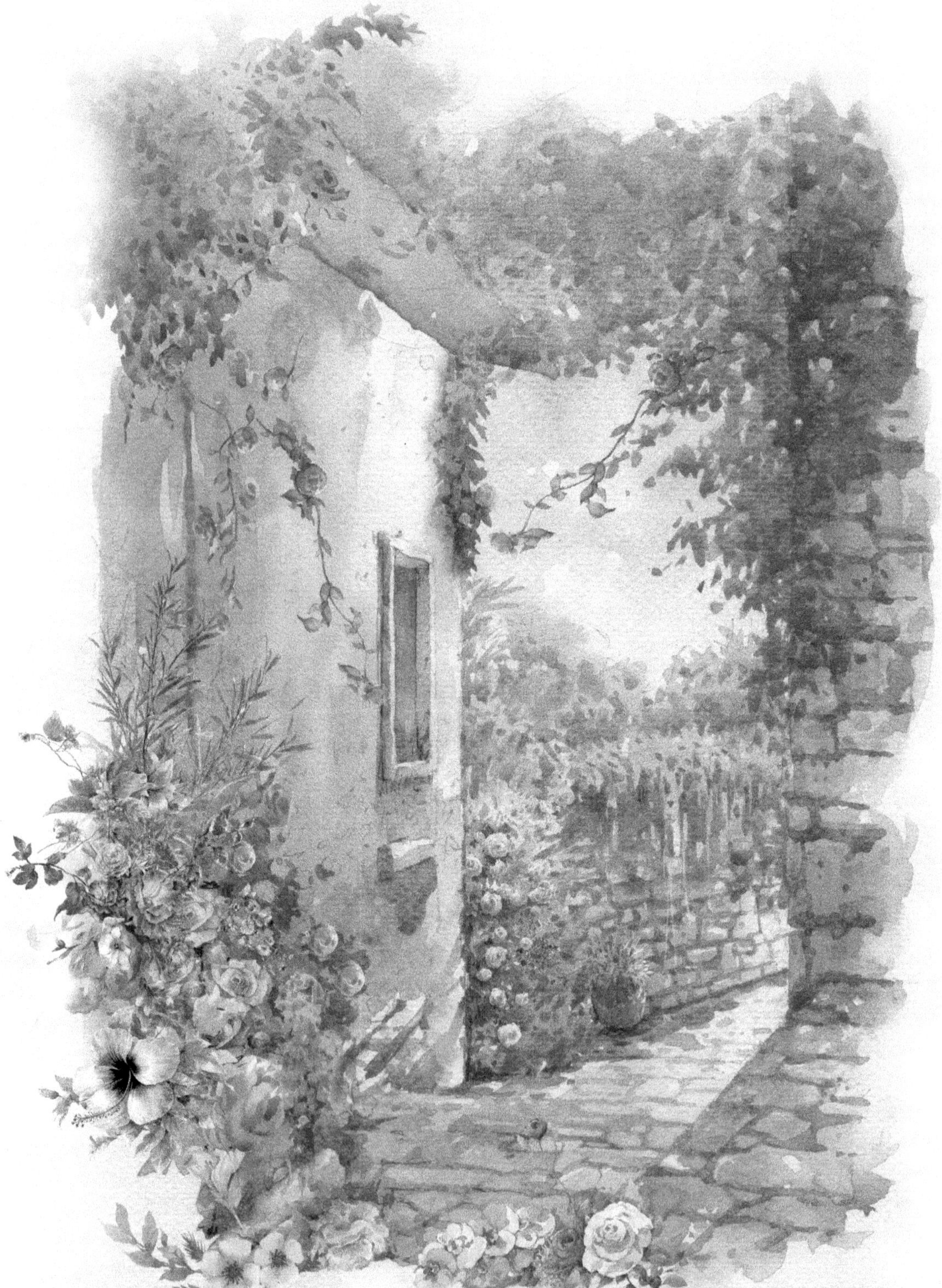

After You have Suffered

AFTER YOU HAVE SUFFERED A LITTLE WHILE,
YOU MAY HEAR YOURSELF ASKING, "WHO WANTS TO SUFFER
I DON'T, DO YOU?
SUFFER FOR WHAT?
FOR WHOM?
HOW COME?
WHY DO I HAVE TO SUFFER, CAN'T I JUST HAVE FUN?
OR, HOW LONG IS A LITTLE WHILE?
OK. LET'S HURRY AND GET IT DONE.
WAIT, WAIT, WHAT ARE WE TALKING ABOUT?
WHAT KIND OF SUFFERING?
I'M BEGINNING TO HAVE MY DOUBTS.

FIRST, LET ME PEER INTO THE LIVES OF OTHERS,
AND SEE WHAT THEY ARE SUFFERING WITH,
AS I SEE THEM, MAYBE I WILL SEE.
HOW THEY GO THROUGH THESE SUFFERINGS,
AND IT'S NOT JUST THINKING ABOUT ME.

By: Maija The Poet

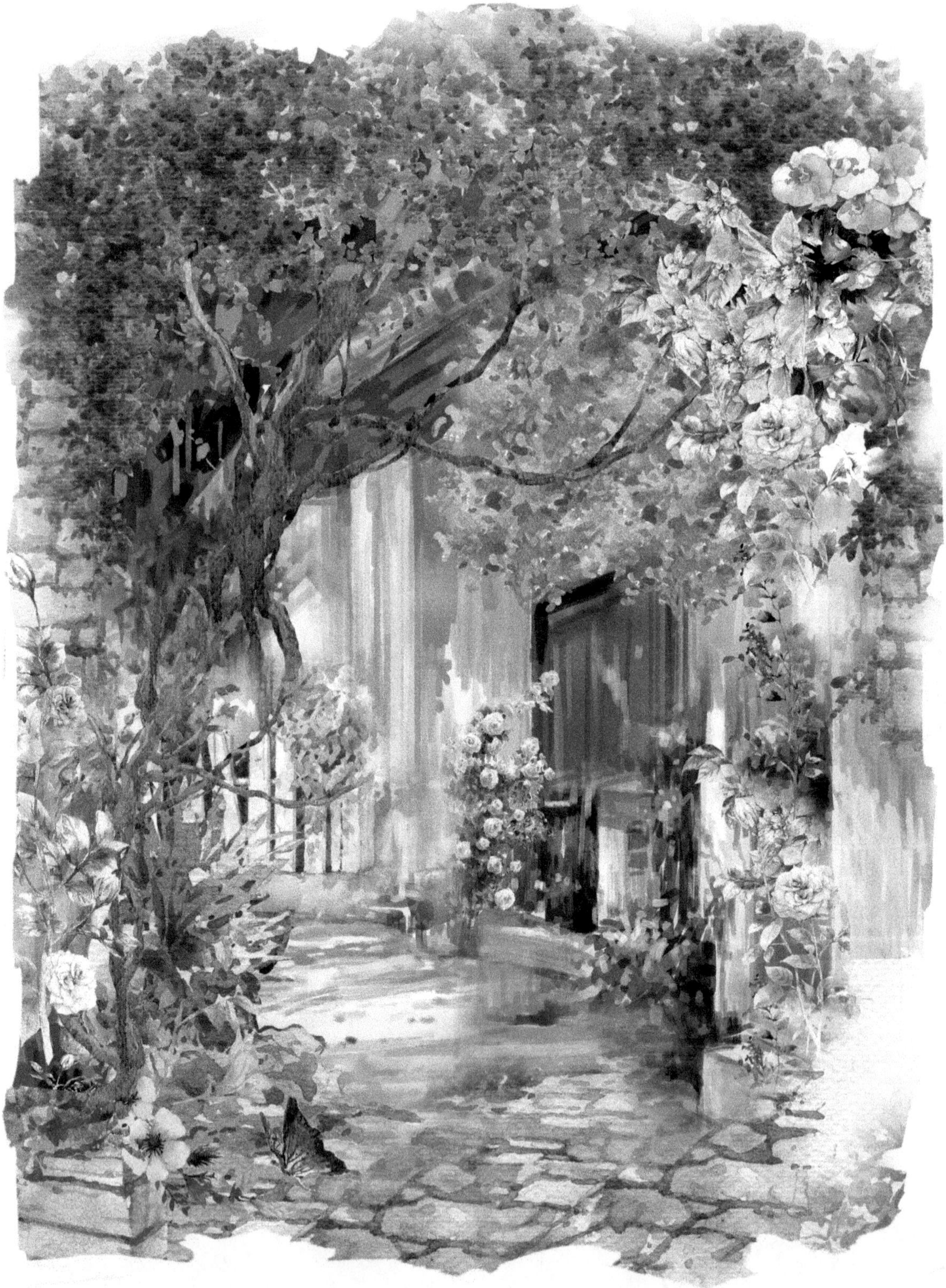

Feelings

I DON'T LIKE FEELINGS, WHEN I FEEL UNLOVED.
OR IGNORED, OR SCREAMED AT, OR CUSSED AT, OR LEFT OUT.

I DON'T LIKE FEELINGS WHEN THEY MAKE YOU FEEL SCARED,
OR INSECURE, OR ALONE, AND UNSURE OF YOURSELF.

I DON'T LIKE THE FEELINGS, WHEN OTHERS TELL LIES ABOUT YOU,
WHEN ALL YOU HAVE DONE IS TRY TO ENCOURAGE.

I WANT TO HAVE FEELINGS OF LOVING OTHERS AND BEING LOVED.
WHY ARE PEOPLE SO EASY TO HATE, DESTROY AND LIE?
INSTEAD OF BUILDING ONE ANOTHER UP?

WHY?

By: Maija The Poet

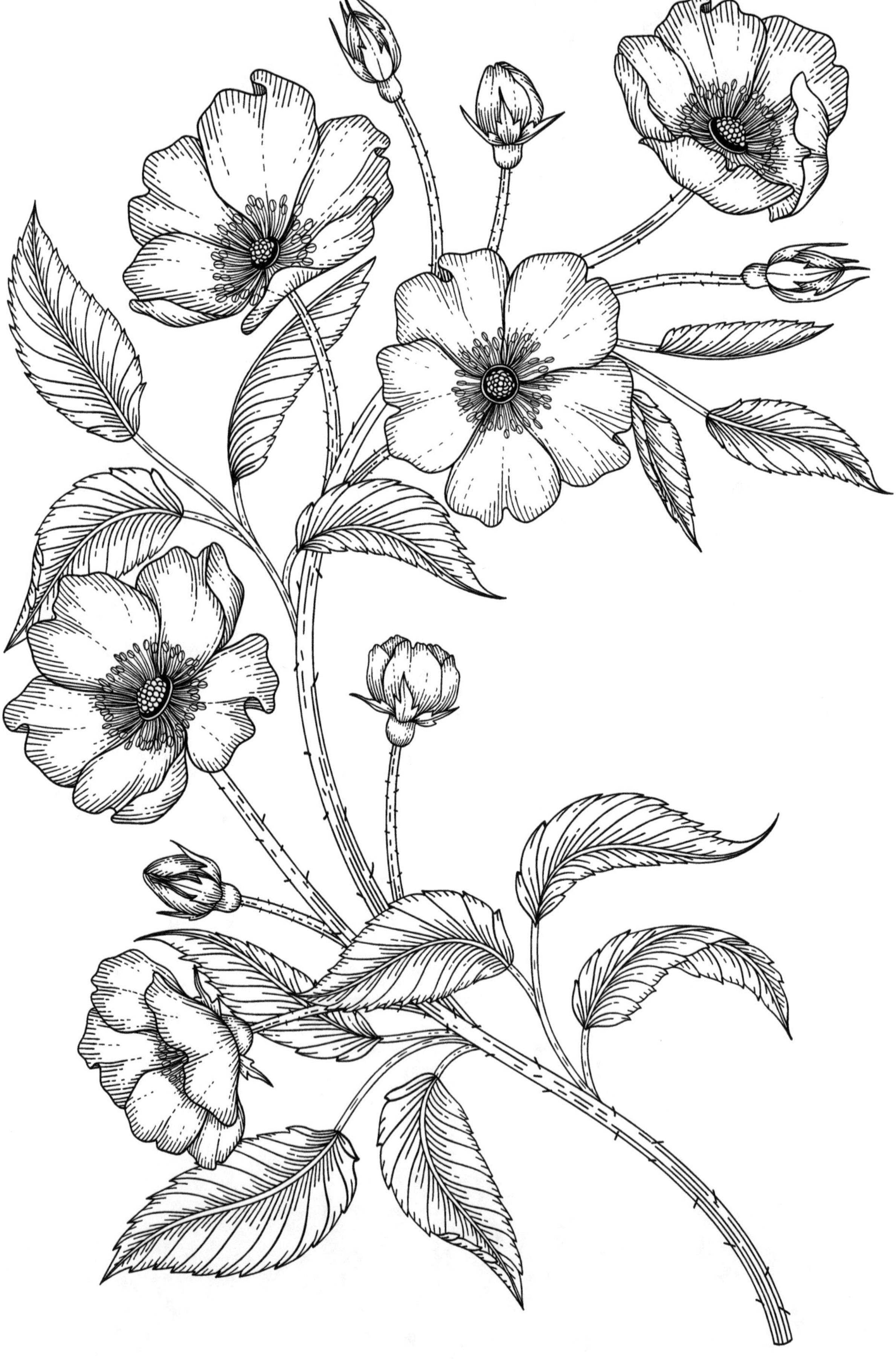

Be Content

BE CONTENT, START TO PLANT,
VISUALIZE ALL I HAVE GIVEN TO YOU.
GIVEN TO YOU, FOR YOU TO DO.
FOR MY GLORY.

BE CONTENT, LOOK OUT AND SEE,
IT IS I, THE GREAT I AM, WHO IS LEADING THEE.
TIME ALONE, TIME AND SPACE,
IS WHAT I AM GIVING YOU AT THIS PLACE.
YOUR HOME WAS DEDICATED TO ME YEARS AGO.

LET'S REFRESH, REDO, AND MAKE IT LIKE NEW.
ANOINT WITH MY OIL, BREATHE DEEPLY IN ME,
MY HOLY SPIRIT WILL LEAD THEE, ALWAYS TO ME.
I LOVE YOU MY DAUGHTER, MY CHILD, AND MY BRIDE,
I AM ANSWERING YOUR PRAYERS,
TO MAKE A HOME FOR YOU HERE.

HERE IS MY HEART, MY JOY AND MY PEACE.
I LOVE YOU MY MARY, NOW PLEASE BE AT EASE.
IN JESUS NAME, AND GLORY TO THE FATHER.
PEACE BE UNTO YOU,
MY PEACE I GIVE TO YOU.

By: Maija The Poet

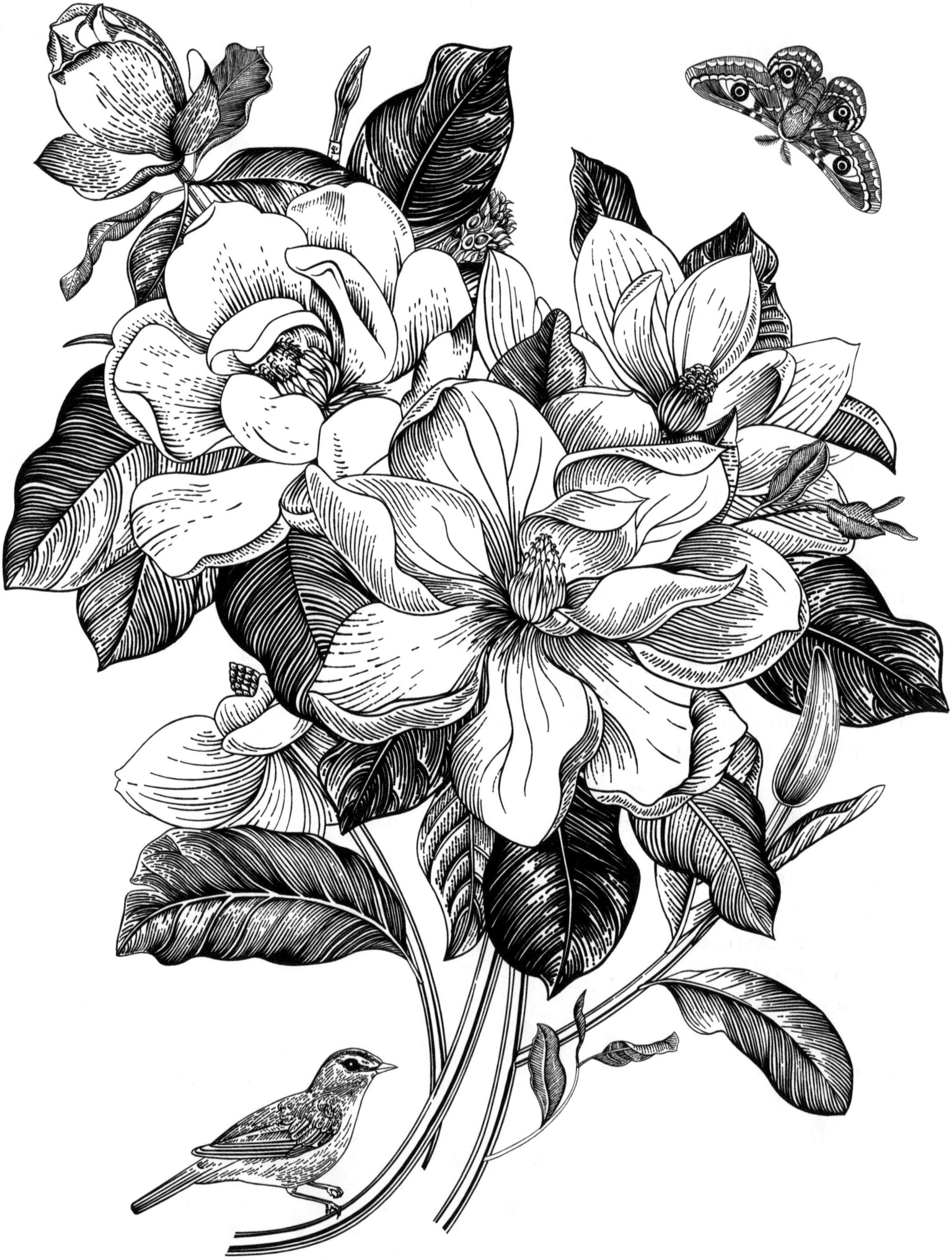

Embrace Freedom

FREE NOW! NO SCHEDULES EXCEPT FOR MY PURPOSE, GOD'S PURPOSE.
GOD CALLING ME TO HIMSELF, TO DO HIS WILL, HIS WAY, AND FOR HIS GLORY!
SET APART, SET ASIDE, SLOW AND SIMPLE, PEACE AND CLARITY OF VOICES.
LISTEN TO MYSELF, LISTEN TO MY BODY, LISTEN TO MY FEELINGS,
I WANT TO BE FREE, I WANT TO BE ME, ALWAYS DOING FOR OTHERS,
I'M TIRED AND BURNED OUT, AND THE TO DO LIST TRULY BOTHERS.
I NEED TIME TO THINK, TO SEE AND TO DO,
SO MANY YEARS OF TAKING CARE OF THE CHILDREN AND THE HOMEFRONT,
AND ALL OF THE OTHER SCHEDULES.

TO TAKE CARE OF ONESELF, IS QUITE A CHALLENGING STUNT.
I LIKE MY QUIET, NO LOUD NOISES,
I CERTAINLY AM NOT LIKE ONE OF THE GOOD OLD BOYS.
TIME TO PLAN, TO THINK AND TO WRITE,
WILL I EVER GET TO FINISH MY BOOK, OR IS IT OUT OF SIGHT?
HELP ME LORD TO TAILOR MY DAYS,
SO, MY QUIET TIME WITH YOU, REMAINS NUMBER ONE ALWAYS.

YOU MUST BE FIRST, FOREVER MY LORD.
KEEP ME ALWAYS IN YOUR WORD.
TEACH ME, GUIDE ME, HELP ME TO BE,
YOUR DAUGHTER WHO WILL ALWAYS WANT TO BE FREE.
FREE TO BE ME. FOR YOUR GLORY!

By Maija The Poet

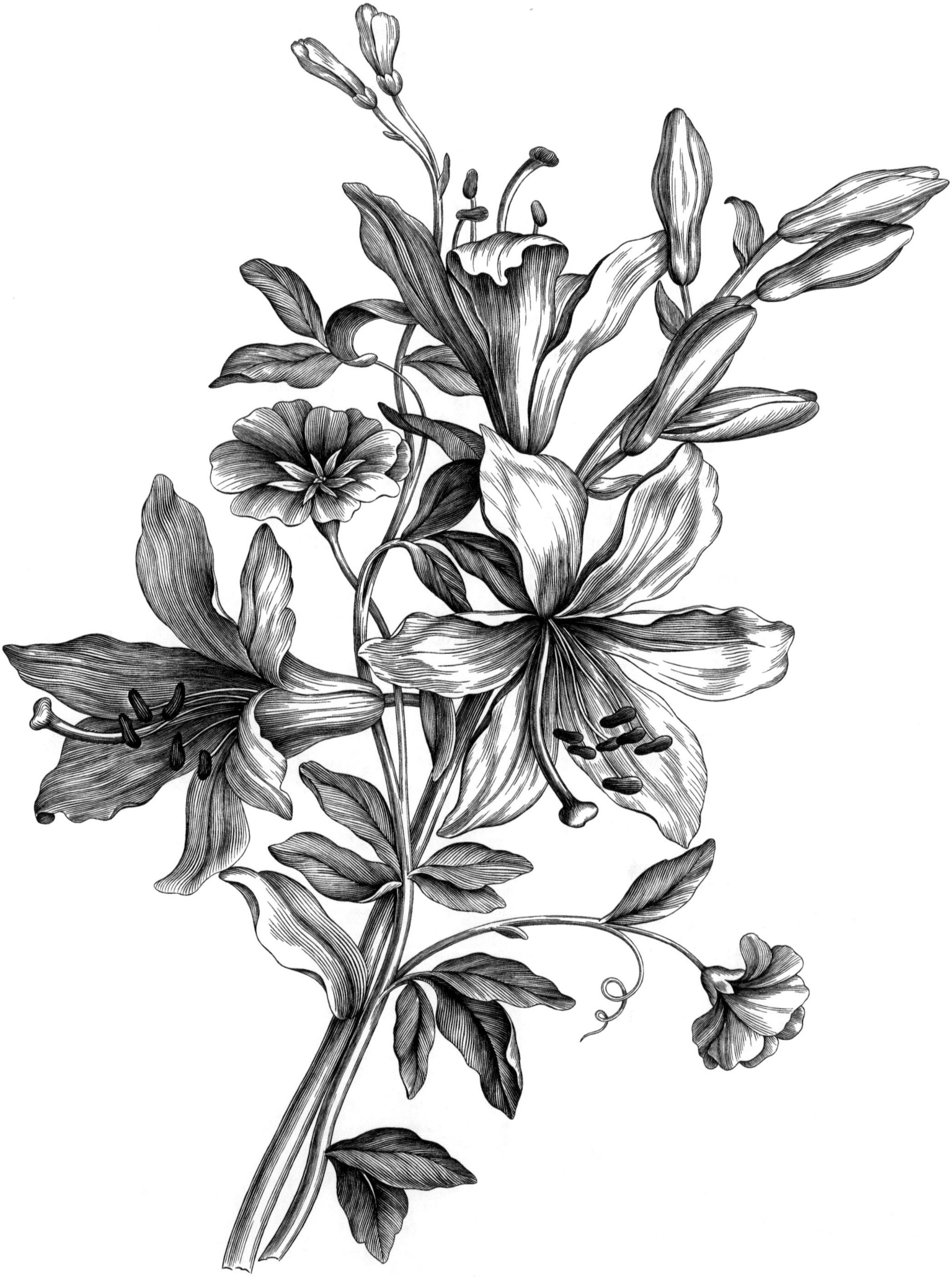

The Lord is my Husband

THE LORD IS MY HUSBAND, I SHALL NOT WANT.
I GIVE UP ALL TO LOVE AND TO SERVE YOU MY FIRST AND LAST LOVE.
I AM WILLING TO LAY DOWN ALL TO FULFILL YOUR PURPOSE FOR MY LIFE.
HELP ME TO ENDURE TO THE END AND TO REMAIN FAITHFUL TO YOU.
GOD YOU ARE A LOVING HUSBAND. GOD, YOU RESTORE MY DIGNITY AND FREEDOM.
GOD DOES NOT ABUSE ME.

IN THAT DAY, DECLARES THE LORD,
YOU WILL CALL ME "MY HUSBAND" YOU WILL NO LONGER CALL ME "MY MASTER". HOSEA 2:16

FOR YOUR HUSBAND IS YOUR MAKER, WHOSE NAME IS THE LORD OF HOSTS,
AND YOUR REDEEMER IS THE HOLY ONE OF ISRAEL,
WHO IS CALLED THE GOD OF ALL THE EARTH. ISAIAH 54:5

I AM JEALOUS FOR YOU WITH A GODLY JEALOUSY. I PROMISED YOU TO ONE HUSBAND,
TO CHRIST, SO THAT I MIGHT PRESENT YOU AS A PURE VIRGIN TO HIM. 2 COR.11:2

JESUS IS ALSO CALLED THE BRIDEGROOM. REV. 19:7, REV.21:9

HELP ME NOT TO FAIL IN WHAT YOU WANT ME TO DO. HELP ME TO DO YOUR WILL.
HELP ME TO LOVE YOU WITH AN EVERLASTING LOVE.

KEEP ME AWAY FROM HUMAN WANTINGS FOR COMFORT AND LOVING FROM
THE EARTHLY HUSBAND YOU GAVE ME.
KEEP ME FROM TEMPTATION.
KEEP ME FOCUSED,
KEEP ME FOCUSED TO TYPE UP THE POEMS AND THE BOOKS YOU HAVE GIVEN TO ME.
IN JESUS NAME, HELP ME LORD, TO KEEP MY EYES, AND MY HEART, ONLY FOR YOU.
FOR YOU AND YOU ALONE.
HELP ME TO FULFILL YOUR PURPOSE, FOR YOUR GLORY.
IN JESUS NAME.

By Maija The Poet

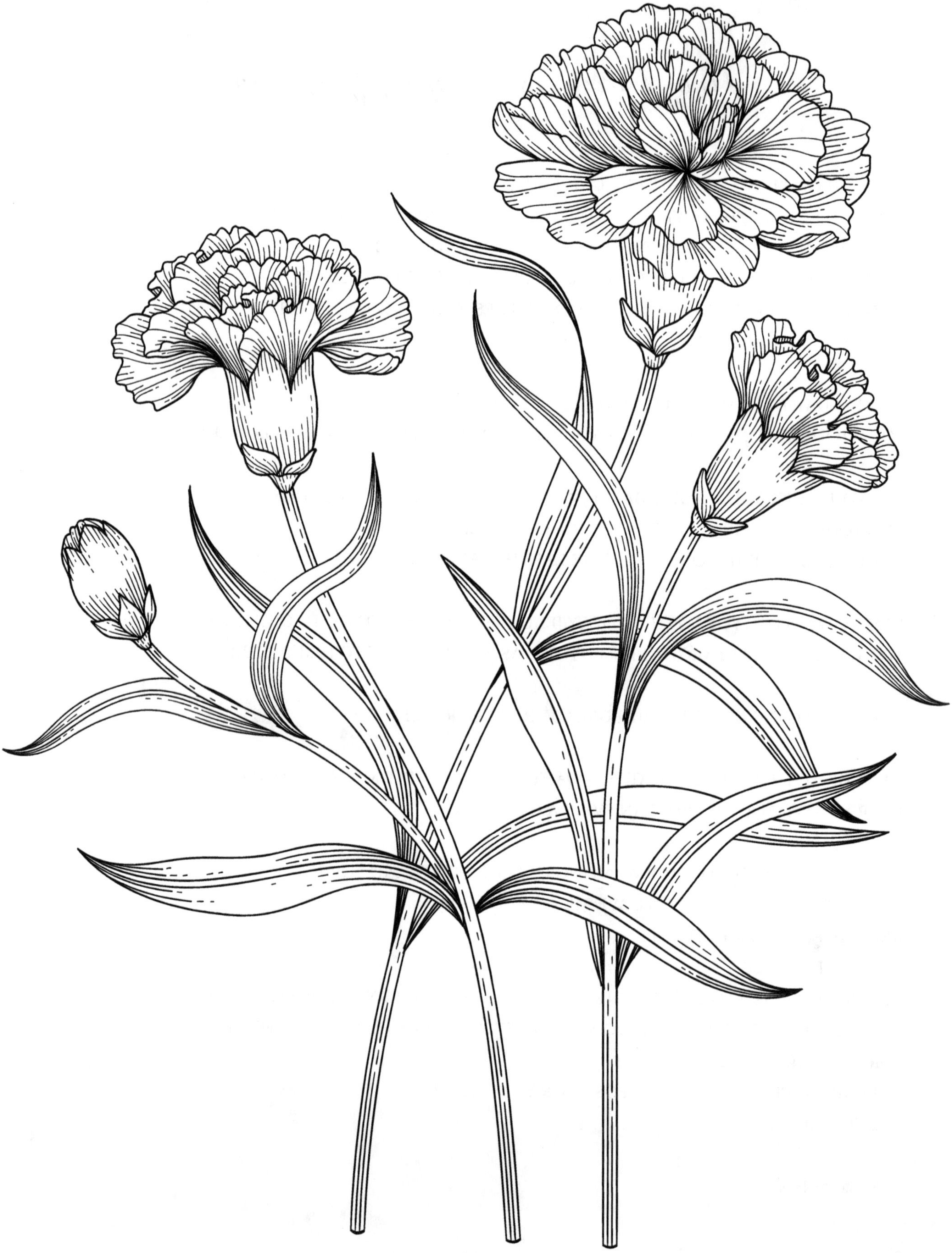

As Jesus Looks Down

AS JESUS LOOKS DOWN UPON THE EARTH,
HE CANNOT SEE ANY DIFFERENCE BETWEEN THOSE WHO BELIEVE,
AND THOSE WHO DO NOT.

WHAT HAS HAPPENED TO MY LOVED ONES?
THEY HAVE TURNED INTO THE WORLD,
AND NOW THEY HAVE BEEN CAUGHT.
IT HAS TAKEN THEM LITTLE BY LITTLE,
UNTIL THEY HAVE FORGOTTEN,
HOW TO HAVE THEIR QUIET TIME DAILY WITH ME,
AND READING AND HEARING MY WORDS AS THEY OUGHT.
DOES IT ALWAYS HAVE TO BE HURRICANES, AND OR BAD NEWS,
BEFORE THEY TURN TO ME?
WHO, OR WHAT DO THEY ALWAYS CHOOSE?
SELF, THE WORLD, SIN, HARDLY EVER ME.

I LOVE ALL, BUT SO FEW RESPOND TO MY CALL.
IT IS A FREE CHOICE, FREE WILL FOR ALL.
I GIVE ETERNAL LIFE, NOT HELL.
TURN TO ME, WHEN I CALL, HEAR MY STILL SMALL VOICE, I REACH OUT TO ALL.
KNOW THAT I LOVE YOU, PLEASE DO NOT FALL.
DON'T FALL INTO UNBELIEF, BUT BELIEVE,
IT IS I CALLING YOU, OH WHAT A RELIEF.
COME INTO MY ARMS, BE WITH ME.
I WILL ALWAYS LOVE YOU TIL ETERNITY.
YOUR FATHER, YOUR CREATOR, YOUR SAVIOR,
IT IS ME.

By: Maija The Poet-Vincent-Mikkola-Babun